JUICES

& SMOOTHIES

JUICES
& SMOOTHIES

Over 200 delicious recipes

hamlyn

An Hachette Livre UK Company

First published in Great Britain in 2008 by Hamlyn,
a division of Octopus Publishing Group Ltd,
2–4 Heron Quays, London E14 4JP
www.octopusbooks.co.uk

ISBN 978-0-600-61734-1

A CIP catalogue record for this book is available
from the British Library

Printed and bound in China

10 9 8 7 6 5 4 3 2 1

Notes
This book includes drinks made with nuts and nut derivatives.
It is advisable for those with known allergic reactions to
nuts and nut derivatives and those who may be potentially
vulnerable to these allergies, such as pregnant and nursing
mothers, invalids, the elderly, babies and children, to avoid
dishes made with nuts and nut oils. It is also prudent to check
the labels of preprepared ingredients for the possible inclusion
of nut derivatives.

Both metric and imperial measurements are given for the
recipes. Use one set of measures only, not a mixture of both.

The calorific values given for each drink is for a single
serving; this is usually 150–200 ml (5–7 fl oz). These values
are a guide only because the weight and size of fruits and
vegetables varies.

contents

introduction

The healthy option

Our lifestyles may have become more hectic, but we have also become increasingly aware of what we eat and of the benefits of a properly balanced diet. Juices and smoothies provide the ideal solution for busy, health-conscious people, being easy to make and packed with healthful ingredients. They have become popular in recent years, juice bars have opened up all over the world and ready-made versions have appeared on supermarket shelves. Many people have switched from buying coffee to drink on their way to work to enjoying instead a healthy juice.

Rather than relying on caffeine for an early-morning energy lift, you can enjoy the benefits that a fresh juice or smoothie provides, while getting a good share of your daily five portions of fruit and vegetables. A juice or smoothie can provide a real boost and is the perfect kick-start to the day. They provide an efficient way of enjoying fruit and vegetables, and they are often low in fat and free from artificial sweeteners, colours and flavourings, so your body is getting nothing but goodness.

Spot the difference

Although the basic idea of a blended fruit or vegetable drink can apply to both juices and smoothies, there are some essential differences between the two. As a rule, extracting the juice from different types of fruit or vegetables creates a juice, to which other ingredients or flavours may then be added – a vitamin shot or a flavoured syrup, for example.

Smoothies, on the other hand, contain whole, puréed fruit or vegetables – the skin and pips are usually included – and they tend, therefore, to have a thicker consistency, because the pulp and fibre are part of the drink. They may also contain milk, yogurt or ice cream as a base ingredient, which also tends to make them thicker.

Obviously, there are many exceptions to the general rule, and, as you will see from the recipes in this book, there is such a huge variety in the combinations of ingredients and flavours that you can create a different drink for every possible mood and occasion.

The ultimate health kick

If you are looking for a quick vitamin boost, you can't go too far wrong with a freshly prepared juice or smoothie. The great thing about these drinks is that you don't necessarily have to go out shopping. As long as you have a few pieces of fruit or some fresh vegetables in your kitchen, you will be able to create a delicious juice or smoothie that's packed full of goodness.

We should all by now be aware of the fact that we are supposed to eat at least five portions of fruit and vegetables a day. Despite all those good intentions, however, it's not always possible to achieve this. Long days in the office, a busy social life or a young family can mean that there's simply not enough time to think about your diet throughout the day, and there will be times when you might end up grabbing something to eat as and when you can.

Again, a freshly made juice or smoothie can help resolve the dilemma, and you could easily pack two or more servings of fruit or vegetables into a drink that takes just minutes to prepare. If you include dairy produce or some grains in your smoothie, it can make a suitable alternative to breakfast. Not only will it be both filling and nutritious, but it will also save a few precious minutes, which you might prefer to spend in bed or under the shower.

Vital vitamins

The vitamin content in many types of fruit and vegetable can deteriorate quite rapidly once it has been harvested, and, in order to maximize the benefits obtained from your juice or smoothie, you should use produce that's as fresh as possible. Try not to buy lots of ingredients infrequently. Instead, aim to buy little and often, incorporating shopping time into other activities, such as travelling to work or dropping the children off at school. This might mean being a little more organized, but once you get into the habit of buying only what you need every couple of days you should find that you waste less and that it becomes easier to plan daily meals. It also means that you can take full advantage of seasonal produce and choose the fruit and vegetables that look the best on the day of purchase.

Juice for immunity

By eating plenty of fresh, raw fruit and vegetables you are maximizing your vitamin and mineral intake, and this will be a great boost to your immune system. A long shelf-life and some cooking techniques can reduce the benefits provided by fresh produce, which is why juices and smoothies are so popular with people who participate in a lot of physical activities. Liquids are more quickly digested by the body than solid food, so you will reap the benefits from a fruit juice or smoothie far more quickly. In addition, by combining a number of different types of fruit and vegetables in a drink, you can choose which vitamins in particular you wish to consume in larger quantities.

Feeling fruity

When it comes to creating tasty juices and smoothies, there are very few fruit or vegetables that cannot successfully be pulped or have their juice extracted. Moreover, while the thought of a plate of pineapple and parsnip might not get your taste buds tingling in anticipation, unusual combinations such as this work very well in a drink (see Parsnip and pineapple, page 217).

In the recipes that follow, you will see all manner of everyday and exotic ingredients. There are, however, a number of firm favourites that appear in many different drinks. Here is a round-up of some of the best fruit and vegetables to use.

Apple

Apples are full of antioxidants and have a naturally sweet flavour that complements sour or savoury ingredients really well.

Apricot

You can use dried apricots, a good store-cupboard staple. They have a high beta-carotene and potassium content.

Avocado

Avocados are full of protein, so any drink containing these will be filling and nutritious. They also contain vitamin E, which makes them beneficial to the skin.

Banana

Bananas provide carbohydrates, making them good for creating a more filling drink, and they also add a rich, sweet flavour and texture.

Beetroot

A great source of folic acid, beetroot also has a high fibre content and is often combined with citrus fruit to create delicious, colourful juices.

Carrot

Carrots are full of beta-carotene. They work well in juices because they have a sweet taste and a vibrant colour.

Celery

Celery sticks provide a good yield of juice, and this vegetable is great for cleansing the digestive system.

Ginger

Renowned by many as an immunity booster, ginger can help fight bugs with its high level of zinc. It also adds a zingy taste to drinks.

Lemon

Lemons are another natural bug buster and combine well with ginger for a natural cold remedy. They are high in vitamin C, a great antioxidant.

Mango

Mango adds an exotic flavour, but it also contains a lot of vitamin C. With a high fibre and potassium content as well, it's a great fruit to keep on your shopping list.

Orange

Oranges are a great source of vitamin C, and these are another popular ingredient in both juices and smoothies.

Peach

This sweet fruit can help to tackle stomach problems with its antioxidant qualities and vitamin C content.

Spinach

Some people will recoil at drinking spinach, but don't knock it till you've tried it. Rich in iron and beta-carotene, this is a great choice for vegetarians.

Strawberry

Beneficial and tasty! Make the most of freshly picked seasonal strawberries, with their high vitamin C content.

Tomato

Tomatoes are believed to help lower the risk of certain cancers, and this is attributed to their lycopene content. They are also high in vitamin C and fibre.

How to make juices and smoothies

If you are just starting out on the road to regular juice and smoothie creation, don't rush into buying any expensive equipment. It's a good idea to think about the types of drink you will probably be making most often and then choose the equipment that will enable you to make those recipes.

Smoothie recipes can generally be made with a blender or food processor because the whole fruit is used. However, if you are planning to make a lot of juices you should consider investing in a decent juicer.

✳ Equipment

There are a number of different types of juicer available, and your choice will really depend on how much you are willing to spend and how efficient you want your juicer to be. For a first foray into the world of juicing, you should be able to create a variety of delicious drinks using nothing more complicated than a simple glass or plastic hand-held orange juicer. This works for all citrus fruit and will give you an idea of whether you want to proceed to more exotic recipes and invest in more sophisticated equipment.

If you do decide to go ahead and buy a juicer, there are two basic options: a masticating juicer, which forces the ingredients through a thin wire mesh to extract as much juice as possible; and a centrifugal type, which uses spinning blades to separate the pulp from the juice. The centrifugal juicer actually produces less juice, but it is a cheaper option, which will be an important consideration if you are on a budget.

✳ Preparing the ingredients

1 Gather all the ingredients together before you begin.

2 Don't prepare the fruit and vegetables for your juice or smoothie until you're ready to make it, because many of them — bananas and avocados, for example — will begin to discolour or deteriorate once they have been peeled or cut.

3 Wash any ingredients that are to be used whole and quickly scrub root vegetables, such as parsnips, carrots and beetroot.

4 Peel (if necessary), core, deseed and roughly chop all the fruit and vegetable ingredients, being careful not to lose any of the juice in the process. The weights given in the recipes that follow are for the amount of prepared fruit or vegetable — for example, pineapple should be skinned and the tough core removed before the given quantity is added to the other ingredients.

✳ Chill out

We have already mentioned the benefits of using the freshest possible ingredients, but some fruit can be successfully frozen and added directly to the blender when you are making smoothies. Freezing is a good way of preserving the vitamin content of food, and it's a really good method of storing seasonal produce, such as strawberries and raspberries, which you can then enjoy all year round. Another fruit that freezes well is, perhaps surprisingly, the banana. Chop the bananas into slices and store in a freezer-proof container, then just take out what you need. The other advantage of adding frozen ingredients to a smoothie is that they will act as a natural chilling element to the drink, thereby avoiding the need for ice, which can sometimes dilute the flavours.

Store-cupboard basics

There are a few ingredients that you should keep in your store cupboard if you think you might get the juice and smoothie bug in a big way. Obviously, you will need to have a good supply of your favourite fresh fruit and vegetables, but keep your refrigerator, freezer and larder well stocked with some of the following essentials.

Milk

Whether it's the full-fat, semi-skimmed or fat-free version, you will need a good supply of milk if you plan to make smoothies. It's an essential ingredient in many recipes. Alternatively, soya milk can often be used if you prefer the taste or are lactose intolerant.

Yogurt

Another popular ingredient in smoothie recipes, natural yogurt is a good staple. However, fruit-flavoured yogurts or frozen yogurt can also be included in some recipes.

✱ Ice cream

Keep some vanilla ice cream in the freezer for those days when you really need to spoil yourself with one of those decadent smoothies that doubles up as a treat.

✱ Honey

Often used as a natural sweetener in juices and smoothies, clear honey dissolves more easily than sugar and adds a gorgeous flavour to all manner of recipes.

✱ Fruit juice

If you run out of fresh fruit or need to top up a drink quickly, fruit juice is a pretty good alternative. Orange or apple juice is most likely to be used, and you should always remember to buy the pure juice, rather than the juice that is made from concentrate.

juices

Grapefruit
and orange

Makes 200 ml (7 fl oz)

1 large **orange**

½ **grapefruit**

1 **lime**

ice cubes or sparkling **mineral water**

This refreshing, tangy juice will give you a real shot of vitamin C and will certainly wake you up in the morning.

1 Peel all the fruit, leaving a little of the pith on the segments. If you like, reserve some of the lime rind to decorate.

2 Juice the fruit, then either serve it over ice or, if you want a longer drink, dilute it with an equal amount of sparkling mineral water.

3 Serve decorated with curls of lime rind, if liked.

155 Kcals

vit C

refresh

Melon and blackberry

The powerful ingredients in this juice will give a great antioxidant punch that will put the colour back in your cheeks.

1 Remove the skin and seeds from the melon and chop the flesh into chunks.

2 Juice the melon, blackberries and kiwifruit (there is no need to peel them). Transfer the juice to a blender with the apple juice and process with a couple of ice cubes.

3 Pour into a glass and serve immediately, decorated with a few blackberries.

Makes 200 ml (7 fl oz)

100 g (3½ oz) **cantaloupe melon**

100 g (3½ oz) fresh or frozen **blackberries**, plus extra to serve

2 **kiwifruit**

100 ml (3½ fl oz) **apple juice**

ice cubes

182 Kcals

vit A

revive

Strawberry and cucumber

Makes 200 ml (7 fl oz)

100 g (3½ oz) **strawberries**

75 g (3 oz) **galia or honeydew melon**

75 g (3 oz) **cucumber**, plus extra to serve (optional)

ice cubes

Strawberries are a good source of vitamin C and have anti-viral and antibiotic properties, while melon and cucumber rehydrate and cleanse the system. This naturally sweet juice is wonderful if you've been overdoing it and feel below par.

1 Hull the strawberries. Remove the skin and seeds from the melon and chop the flesh into chunks. Juice the fruit with the cucumber.

2 Pour the juice over ice in a tall glass and serve immediately. You can decorate with a few cucumber slices, if liked.

65 Kcals

vit C

energize

Rocket and watercress

This juice is an excellent way to counteract some of the detrimental impacts of prolonged stress on your health, thanks to the avocado. The avocado gives a lovely smoothness to the drink.

1 Trim the celery and cut it into 5 cm (2 inch) pieces, then juice the celery, rocket, watercress and apple.

2 Transfer the juice to a blender with the avocado and a couple of ice cubes and process until smooth. Serve immediately, garnished with a slice of lime, if liked.

Makes 200 ml (7 fl oz)

150 g (5 oz) **celery**

25 g (1 oz) **rocket**

25 g (1 oz) **watercress**

1 **apple**

½ small **avocado**

ice cubes

lime slices, to serve (optional)

267 Kcals

vit E

soothe

Spinach
and celery

Makes 600 ml (1 pint)

2 **oranges**

½ **lemon**

1 cm (½ inch) cube **fresh root ginger**

100 g (3½ oz) **carrots**

100 g (3½ oz) **beetroot**

100 g (3½ oz) **spinach**

100 g (3½ oz) **celery**

This is an absolute 'super juice'. It's a low-calorie, virtually fat-free burst of goodness, which will enliven your whole body. It's great for lowering blood pressure, helping digestion, boosting the immune system and eliminating toxins.

1 Peel the oranges and the lemon. If you like, reserve some of the orange rind to garnish. Peel and chop the ginger and scrub the carrots and beetroot. Prepare the celery as on page 23. Juice all the ingredients.

2 Pour the juice into a large glass and serve garnished with curls of orange rind, if liked.

286 Kcals

low-cal

refresh

24 juices

Spinach and broccoli

All the ingredients in this juice are high in magnesium and vitamin C. If you are leading a very hectic life, the chances are that your body will be lacking these two vital nutrients.

1 Trim the broccoli and juice it with the spinach and tomatoes.

2 Pour the juice into a tall glass over ice and serve immediately, garnished with sliced tomatoes, if liked.

Makes 200 ml (7 fl oz)

150 g (5 oz) **broccoli**

150 g (5 oz) **spinach**

2 **tomatoes**, plus extra to serve (optional)

ice cubes

120 Kcals

vit C

calm

Apple and apricot

Makes 200 ml (7 fl oz)

1 **peach**, plus extra to serve (optional)

3 **apricots**

2 **apples**

ice cubes

This cooling juice supplies almost a complete daily quota of beta-carotene, and the apples are superb for lowering blood cholesterol. Make sure that you juice them with the pips, because the pectin helps to remove toxins that may be building up in your body.

1 Cut the peach and apricots in half and remove the stones. Juice the apples with the apricots and peach.

2 Transfer the juice to a blender with a couple of ice cubes and process for 10 seconds.

3 Pour the juice into a tall glass and serve decorated with slices of peach, if liked.

238 Kcals

pectin

calm

Grape and lettuce

Lettuce contains a natural sedative, lactucin, which has a calming effect on the mind and body. Grapes are effective at lowering blood pressure, so make this juice when you feel your pressure levels rising. It has a sharp taste with sweet undertones.

1 Peel and chop the ginger. Juice the grapes and lettuce with the ginger.

2 Pour the juice into a tall glass over ice and serve immediately, decorated with grapes, if liked. Alternatively, transfer it to a blender and process briefly with a couple of ice cubes for a smoother, creamier drink.

Makes 200 ml (7 fl oz)

2.5 cm (1 inch) cube **fresh root ginger**

200 g (7 oz) **white grapes**, plus extra to serve (optional)

200 g (7 oz) **lettuce**

ice cubes

134 Kcals

lactucin

soothe

Celery and pineapple

Makes 200 ml (7 fl oz)

½ **lemon**

150 g (5 oz) **pineapple**

150 g (5 oz) **celery**

sprigs of **mint**, to serve (optional)

ice cubes

Pineapple contains bromelin, an enzyme that aids digestion. Celery is the perfect accompaniment as it also aids digestion and lowers blood pressure. This juice is good for re-energizing, detoxifying your body and replenishing lost fluids.

1 Peel the lemon and cut the pineapple into chunks. Trim and cut the celery into 5 cm (2 inch) pieces. Juice the celery, lemon and pineapple.

2 Pour the juice into a tall glass over ice and serve garnished with sprigs of mint, if liked.

101 Kcals

vit B

detox

Fennel and camomile

If you are worried about something, take five minutes to relax and enjoy this soothing juice. Fennel has anti-spasmodic properties, and when it is combined with naturally calming camomile tea it should settle even the most nervous of stomachs.

1 Peel the lemon and juice it with the fennel. Mix the juice with the camomile tea.

2 Pour the juice into a tall glass over ice and serve with slices of lemon, if liked.

Makes 200 ml (7 fl oz)

1 **lemon**, plus extra to serve (optional)

150 g (5 oz) **fennel**

100 ml (3½ fl oz) chilled **camomile tea**

ice cubes

55 Kcals

vit C

soothe

Pepper and papaya

Makes 200 ml (7 fl oz)

100 g (3½ oz) **red pepper**, plus extra to serve (optional)

about 125 g (4 oz) **papaya**

1 large **tomato**

ice cubes

When you are stressed, you will often find that your digestion and circulation are affected, leaving you feeling tired and lacking in energy. Red peppers are excellent for reducing blood pressure, while papaya is renowned for its digestive properties.

1 Core and deseed the red pepper and remove the skin and seeds from the papaya. Juice the tomato with the pepper and papaya flesh.

2 Transfer the juice to a blender, add a couple of ice cubes and process for a few seconds.

3 Pour the juice into a tall glass and serve decorated with slivers of red pepper, if liked.

124 Kcals

vit C

revive

Apple and lettuce

A natural tranquillizer, lettuce contains small amounts of lactucin, which is known to induce a state of relaxation. Apple, in addition to being packed full of nutrients, gives this juice a comforting natural sweetness.

1 Juice the lettuce and apple.

2 Pour the juice into a tall glass over ice and serve immediately, decorated with slices of apple, if liked.

Makes 200 ml (7 fl oz)

175 g (6 oz) cos (romaine) **lettuce**

1 **apple**, about 250 g (8 oz), plus extra to serve (optional)

ice cubes

71 Kcals

fibre

calm

Orange and sweet potato

Makes 200 ml (7 fl oz)

2 small **oranges**

150 g (5 oz) **carrots**

150 g (5 oz) **sweet potato**

sprigs of **mint**, to serve (optional)

ice cubes (optional)

If you are feeling the dual effects of burning the midnight oil and eating too much junk food, this is the ideal juice.

1 Peel the oranges and scrub the carrots. Juice the sweet potato with the oranges and carrots.

2 Pour the juice into a tall glass and serve garnished with sprigs of mint, if liked. Alternatively, transfer the juice to a blender and process briefly with a couple of ice cubes to make a smoother, creamier drink.

358 Kcals

vit A

revive

Orange and carrot

This juice is full of vitamins A and C, which should help keep colds at bay, and it also contains magnesium and zinc. All citrus fruit are invaluable when you have a winter cold.

1 Peel the oranges, leaving on as much pith as possible, and scrub the carrots. Juice the carrots with the oranges.

2 Pour the juice into a tall glass and serve it immediately.

Makes 200 ml (7 fl oz)

2 **oranges**

125 g (4 oz) **carrots**

188 Kcals

zinc

boost

Orange and kiwifruit

Makes 200 ml (7 fl oz)

2 **oranges**

200 g (7 oz)
strawberries

1 **kiwifruit**

This juice packs a mighty antiviral punch, as it is bursting with vitamin C. Kiwifruit are packed with antioxidants, among which are high levels of vitamins C and E – in fact, they contain more vitamin C than oranges do.

1 Peel the oranges, leaving on as much pith as possible, and hull the strawberries. Juice the kiwifruit (there is no need to peel it) with the oranges and strawberries, reserving some strawberries for decoration.

2 Pour the juice into a tall glass and serve immediately, decorated with the reserved strawberries.

201 Kcals

vit C

revive

Apple and celery

This simple and refreshing juice is an invaluable immune booster. The soluble fibre in apples, pectin, helps to lower blood cholesterol levels and is also beneficial for the digestive system.

1 Trim the celery and cut it into 5 cm (2 inch) lengths. Juice it with the tomatoes and apple.

2 Pour the juice into a glass over ice, stir in the chopped basil and lime juice and serve immediately.

Makes 200 ml (7 fl oz)

1 **celery stick**

4 large **tomatoes**

1 **apple**

ice cubes

4 **basil leaves**, finely chopped

1½ tablespoons **lime juice**

203 Kcals

vit A

boost

Red pepper and mango

Makes 200 ml (7 fl oz)

125 g (4 oz) **strawberries**

125 g (4 oz) **watermelon**

1 **mango**

100 g (3½ oz) **red pepper**

50 g (2 oz) **tomatoes**

2–3 **ice cubes**

This drink is bursting with beta-carotene, which is converted into vitamin A in the body. All peppers, especially red ones, contain high levels of beta-carotene, but they also contain the antioxidants vitamin C, vitamin E and zinc – essential for fighting off free radicals.

1 Hull the strawberries. Remove the skin and, if you want, the seeds from the watermelon. Peel and remove the stone from the mango, and transfer 125 g (4 oz) flesh to the juicer. If you like, reserve a few slices of mango to garnish. Juice the pepper and tomatoes with the strawberries, watermelon and mango.

2 Transfer the juice to a blender or food processor and process briefly with the ice cubes.

3 Pour the juice into a tall glass and serve garnished with the reserved mango slices, if liked.

200 Kcals

zinc

revive

Kiwifruit and pear

Like apples, pears are great for ridding the body
of toxins, and will help to cleanse your digestive
system and clear your skin.

1 Wash the pears, peel the kiwifruit and scrub
the lime. Cut the fruit into evenly sized pieces
and juice them.

2 Pour the juice into a glass, add a couple of ice
cubes and serve immediately, decorated with slices
of kiwifruit, if liked.

Makes 300 ml (½ pint)

2 ripe **pears**

3 **kiwifruit**, plus extra to
serve (optional)

½ **lime**

ice cubes

210 Kcals

vit C

boost

Cabbage
and tomato

Makes 200 ml (7 fl oz)

200 g (7 oz) **cabbage**

100 g (3½ oz) **tomatoes**, plus extra to serve

large handful of **parsley**

1 **celery stick**, to serve (optional)

This juice will give your system a boost if you are feeling sluggish. Cabbage is most powerful when it is raw, as it improves digestion, stimulates the immune system and is a natural antioxidant. Parsley is also a natural breath freshener.

1 Separate the cabbage leaves and juice them with the tomatoes and parsley.

2 Pour the juice into a tall tumbler, garnish with sliced tomatoes and serve with a stick of celery, if liked.

77 Kcals

folic acid

refresh

Grapefruit
and celery

This is a brilliant juice for detoxifying your system. Celery helps to flush out toxins and rehydrate your body, while the fennel helps to digest fat and will give your liver a break. Grapefruit is a powerful blood cleanser.

1 Trim the celery and cut it into 5 cm (2 inch) lengths. Peel the grapefruit and juice it with the celery and fennel.

2 Pour the juice into a tall glass over ice and serve immediately.

Makes 200 ml (7 fl oz)

100 g (3½ oz) **celery**

½ **grapefruit**

100 g (3½ oz) **fennel**

ice cubes

87
Kcals

vit C

revive

Kiwifruit and orange

Makes 200 ml (7 fl oz)

2 large **oranges**

2 **kiwifruit**

ice cubes

lemon twist

sprig of **mint**

Remember that kiwifruit contain even more vitamin C than oranges, so by combining the two you are giving yourself an extremely potent dose.

1 Peel the oranges, leaving on as much pith as possible, and juice them along with the kiwifruit (there is no need to peel them).

2 Pour the juice into a tall glass over ice and serve garnished with a twist of lemon and a sprig of mint.

40 juices

216 Kcals

vit C

refresh

Pear and cranberry

This extra-light refreshing juice will help to flush out your system. Using a fruit juice makes this particularly easy to prepare.

1 Wash the pear and juice it. Mix the pear juice with the cranberry juice.

2 Pour the juice into a tall glass over ice and serve immediately.

Makes 200 ml (7 fl oz)

1 large **pear**

100 ml (3½ fl oz) **cranberry juice**

ice cubes

153 Kcals

vit A

boost

Spinach
and apple

Makes 200 ml (7 fl oz)

150 g (5 oz) **broccoli**

2 **apples**

150 g (5 oz) **spinach**

ice cubes (optional)

This super juice will give your immune system a real boost. The combination of ingredients produces a delightful green hue to the juice!

1 Trim the broccoli and juice it with the apples and spinach, alternating the spinach leaves with the broccoli and apple to make sure that the machine doesn't get clogged up with the leaves.

2 Pour the juice into a tall glass and serve. Alternatively, transfer it to a blender and process it with a couple of ice cubes before serving.

230 Kcals

folic acid

uplift

Radish
and carrot

Try this wonderfully reviving juice if you are suffering from a bad cold. Carrots contain huge amounts of vitamin A, which is vital for fighting infection.

1 Scrub the carrots. Juice the radishes and apple with the carrots.

2 Transfer the juice to a blender, add a couple of ice cubes and process briefly.

3 Pour the juice into a tall glass and serve immediately.

Makes 200 ml (7 fl oz)

250 g (8 oz) **carrots**

50 g (2 oz) **radishes**

1 large **apple**

ice cubes

178 Kcals

vit A

cleanse

Cranberry and cucumber

Makes 200 ml (7 fl oz)

1 **orange**

50 g (2 oz) **cucumber**

100 ml (3½ fl oz) **cranberry juice**

ice cubes

This lovely, thirst-quenching juice is great if your system needs instant reydration, and helps to replace lost nutrients. Cucumber is wonderful for hydration and cranberries are highly beneficial for the kidneys and bladder.

1 Peel the orange, leaving on as much pith as possible. Juice the cucumber with the orange.

2 Mix the juice with the cranberry juice. Pour the mixture into a tall glass over ice and serve immediately.

119 Kcals

vit C

refresh

Cauliflower and carrot

Cauliflower helps to purify the blood, lowers blood pressure and is a great antioxidant. It does have a distinctive flavour, however; so, if you have a sweet tooth, add an apple to help disguise it.

1 Trim the cauliflower and scrub the carrots. Juice the tomato with the cauliflower and carrots.

2 Pour the juice into a tall glass over ice, if liked, and serve immediately.

Makes 200 ml (7 fl oz)

100 g (3½ oz) **cauliflower**

200 g (7 oz) **carrots**

1 large **tomato**

ice cubes (optional)

139 Kcals

folic acid

cleanse

Carrot
and fennel

Makes 200 ml (7 fl oz)

200 g (7 oz) **carrots**

200 g (7 oz) **fennel**

ice cubes

A glass of this juice should give you an immediate lift and is fabulous for bright eyes and clear skin. Because of their high potassium content, both carrot and fennel are effective detoxifiers. Fennel also helps to digest fats, boosting liver function.

1 Scrub the carrots. Juice the fennel together with the carrots.

2 Pour the juice into a tall glass over ice and serve immediately.

152 Kcals

vit A

detox

Melon fresh

If you want to cleanse and rehydrate your system, melon has a fantastically high water content and replenishes lost fluids, particularly when taken on its own. Cantaloupe melon contains high levels of beta-carotene, vitamin C and potassium. Juice it with the seeds for extra trace elements.

1 Remove the skin from the melon, then juice the seeds and flesh.

2 Pour the juice into a tall glass over ice and serve immediately.

Makes 300 ml (½ pint)

500 g (1 lb)
cantaloupe melon

ice cubes

180 Kcals

vit C

refresh

Apple and pear

Makes 350 ml (12 fl oz)

1 **pear**

2 **oranges**, plus extra to serve (optional)

1 red **apple**

1 teaspoon **clear honey** (optional)

ice cubes

This juice contains large amounts of carbohydrate and the honey gives an extra energy boost, as well as adding a delicious sweetness.

1 Wash the pear. Peel the oranges, leaving on as much pith as possible. Juice the apple with the pear and oranges.

2 Pour the juice into a tall glass and stir in the honey (if used). Add a couple of ice cubes and serve immediately, decorated with slices of orange, if liked.

225 Kcals

copper

boost

Lettuce and camomile

This soothing juice contains lettuce, which is a good source of vitamin A and potassium. For a cleansing effect on your system, substitute the calming camomile tea with the detoxifying powers of dandelion leaf tea.

1 Peel the lemon. Juice the lettuce and lemon, then mix with the camomile tea.

2 Pour the juice into a tall glass over ice and serve with a slice of lemon.

Makes 200 ml (7 fl oz)

½ **lemon**, plus extra to serve

100 g (3½ oz) cos (romaine) **lettuce**

100 ml (3½ fl oz) chilled **camomile tea**

ice cubes

24
Kcals

vit A

calm

Minty celery and celeriac

Makes 200 ml (7 fl oz)

100 g (3½ oz) **celeriac**

100 g (3½ oz) **Jerusalem artichokes**

100 g (3½ oz) **celery**

small bunch of **mint**

ice cubes

Mint is a good source of potassium and combining it with celeriac and celery makes this delicious juice super-rich in potassium. Mint freshens and sweetens your breath.

1 Peel the celeriac and chop it into sticks. Scrub the artichokes. Juice the vegetables and the mint, alternating the mint leaves with the other ingredients to make sure that the machine doesn't get clogged up with the leaves.

2 Transfer the juice to a blender and process briefly with a couple of ice cubes.

3 Pour into a tall glass and serve immediately.

130 Kcals

vit K

revive

Celeriac and beetroot

The juice has quite a bitter taste, so liquidizing it with ice helps to make it more palatable. The detoxing benefits you get from the juice far outweigh the bitterness though.

1 Peel the celeriac and scrub the beetroot and carrots. Cut the root vegetables into evenly sized chunks and process them with the radicchio and apple.

2 Transfer the juice to a blender and process briefly with a couple of ice cubes.

3 Pour the juice into a tall glass and serve immediately.

Makes 200 ml (7 fl oz)

100 g (3½ oz) **celeriac**
50 g (2 oz) **beetroot**
100 g (3½ oz) **carrots**
50 g (2 oz) **radicchio**
1 **apple**
ice cubes

191 Kcals

vit B

cleanse

Carrot and ginger

Makes 250 ml (8 fl oz)

200 g (7 oz) **carrots**

1 cm (½ inch) cube **fresh root ginger**

1 green **apple**

ice cubes

A great juice to help if you are feeling nauseous – ginger will help to alleviate symptoms of nausea, while carrot and apple provide a burst of nutrients. Choose a fairly tart apple, such as Granny Smith, to counterbalance the sweetness of the carrot juice.

1 Scrub the carrots and peel and roughly chop the ginger. Cut the apple and carrots into evenly sized pieces and juice them with the ginger.

2 Pour the juice into a tall glass, add a couple of ice cubes and serve immediately.

127 Kcals

vit A

soothe

Mango and strawberry

This tempting low-fat juice contains calcium, iron and carbohydrate, so it's great for boosting energy and raising iron levels.

1 Hull the strawberries and freeze them for at least 2 hours or overnight.

2 Peel and stone the mango, roughly chop the flesh and place it in a food processor or blender with the frozen strawberries and orange juice. Process until thick and smooth.

3 Pour the juice into a tall glass and serve immediately, decorated with slices of mango, if liked.

Makes 400 ml (14 fl oz)

125 g (4 oz) **strawberries**

1 small ripe **mango**, plus extra to serve (optional)

300 ml (½ pint) **orange juice**

213 Kcals

copper

boost

Apricot and pineapple

Makes 350 ml (12 fl oz)

65 g (2½ oz) ready-to-eat **dried apricots**

350 ml (12 fl oz) **pineapple juice**

ice cubes

Dried apricots are a good source of beta-carotene, potassium and iron, making them useful for refuelling and boosting energy levels. However, some brands of dried apricots are preserved using sulphur dioxide, which can trigger asthma attacks. Check the packaging or rinse the apricots thoroughly before eating them.

1 Roughly chop the apricots and put them in a large bowl. Pour the pineapple juice over them, cover and allow to stand overnight.

2 Transfer the apricots and juice to a blender and process until thick and smooth.

3 Pour the juice into a tall glass, add a couple of ice cubes and serve immediately.

246 Kcals

vit A

energize

Mango and pineapple

This is a good juice to drink after exercise, when you need a boost. It is rich in vitamins, while tasting like an exotic cocktail!

1 Peel and stone the mango. Roughly chop the flesh and freeze it for at least 2 hours or overnight.

2 Put the frozen mango in a blender with the pineapple juice and lime rind and juice and process until thick.

3 Pour the juice into tall glasses and serve immediately, decorated with lime wedges, if liked.

Makes 400 ml (14 fl oz)

1 ripe **mango**

300 ml (½ pint) **pineapple juice**

rind and juice of ½ **lime**, plus extra to serve (optional)

213
Kcals

vit B

boost

Grape and melon

Makes 300 ml (½ pint)

about 150 g (5 oz) **galia melon**

75 g (3 oz) seedless **green grapes**, plus extra to serve (optional)

150 ml (¼ pint) **water**

ice cubes

This juice is particularly suitable when you feel like a really thirst-quenching and energizing drink. It is an excellent source of vitamins C, B1 and B6, copper, magnesium and phosphorus.

1 Remove the skin and seeds from the melon and chop the flesh into chunks. Juice the grapes with the melon.

2 Mix the juice with the water. Pour it into tall glasses over ice and serve immediately, decorated with sliced grapes, if liked.

87 Kcals

vit B

revive

Grape and kiwifruit

This juice will help to get you through the day as it contains large amounts of carbohydrate for energy release, plus a hefty amount of vitamin C.

1 Peel the kiwifruit and juice the flesh with the grapes.

2 Pour the juice into a tall glass, add a couple of ice cubes and serve immediately, decorated with slices of kiwifruit, if liked.

Makes 300 ml (½ pint)

2 **kiwifruit**, plus extra to serve (optional)

300 g (10 oz) seedless **green grapes**

ice cubes

239 Kcals

vit C

boost

Grape and beetroot

Makes 200 ml (7 fl oz)

100 g (3½ oz) **beetroot**

100 g (3½ oz) **plums**

100 g (3½ oz) seedless **red grapes**

ice cubes

This rich and sweet juice is a great blood restorer and liver regenerator – helping it to cleanse and purify your blood effectively.

1 Scrub the beetroot and remove the stones from the plums. Juice the grapes with the beetroot and plums.

2 Pour the juice into a tall glass over ice and serve immediately.

143 Kcals

vit B

restore

Banana and strawberry

This high-carbohydrate, low-fat drink is a great choice if your body needs to refuel. Bananas are high in potassium, a vital mineral for muscle and nerve function.

1 Peel the banana and hull the strawberries. Freeze the fruit for at least 2 hours or overnight.

2 Put the frozen fruit and orange juice into a blender and process until thick and creamy.

3 Pour the juice into a tall glass and serve immediately, decorated with strawberries, if liked.

Makes 200 ml (7 fl oz)

1 small ripe **banana**

50 g (2 oz) **strawberries**, plus extra to serve (optional)

125 ml (4 fl oz) **orange juice**

90 Kcals

vit C

revive

Pineapple
and melon

Makes 300 ml (½ pint)

about 400 g (13 oz) **galia melon**

about 215 g (7½ oz) **pineapple**

1 green **apple**, plus extra to serve (optional)

ice cubes

This juice has quite a high carbohydrate content, so it's ideal for providing energy. Melon and pineapple are both sweet, so choose a tart apple, such as Granny Smith.

1 Remove the skin and seeds from the melon and chop the flesh into chunks. Remove the skin and core from the pineapple. Juice the apple with the melon and pineapple.

2 Pour the juice into tall glasses over ice and serve immediately, decorated with slices of apple, if liked.

216 Kcals

vit C

refresh

Strawberry and redcurrant

This is an excellent summer refresher, especially when the sun-ripened berries are at their most plentiful. Buy extra and freeze them so you can enjoy a little summer sunshine all year round. The calcium and iron content helps to prevent fatigue.

1 Hull the strawberries and redcurrants and peel the orange. Juice the fruit.

2 Mix the juice with the water and stir in the honey (if used).

3 Pour the juice into tall glasses over ice and serve immediately, decorated with redcurrants, if liked.

Makes 250 ml (8 fl oz)

100 g (3½ oz) **strawberries**

75 g (3 oz) **redcurrants**, plus extra to serve (optional)

½ **orange**

125 ml (4 fl oz) **water**

½ teaspoon **clear honey** (optional)

ice cubes

65 Kcals

calcium

boost

Pear and pineapple

Makes 300 ml (½ pint)

2 **pears**

about 215 g (7½ oz)
pineapple, plus extra to
serve (optional)

½ **lime**

ice cubes

This juice is rich in B vitamins, which help to release energy from carbohydrate. The addition of lime should help to counteract too much sweetness in the pears.

1 Wash the pears and remove the skin and tough core of the pineapple. Juice the lime with the pears and pineapple.

2 Pour the juice into tall glasses over ice and serve immediately, decorated with pieces of pineapple, if liked.

211
Kcals

vit C

energize

Mango and passion fruit

This juice is high in natural carbohydrates, making it a wonderful energy provider. To offset the sweetness of the mango, choose fairly tart apples, such as Worcester.

1 Chop the apples into evenly sized pieces. Cut the passion fruit in half, scoop out the flesh and strain to remove the seeds. Peel the mango and remove the stone. Juice the fruit.

2 Pour the juice into a tall glass, add a couple of ice cubes and serve immediately.

Makes 300 ml (½ pint)

3 red **apples**

2 **passion fruit**

1 **mango**

ice cubes

237
Kcals

calcium

boost

Orange and watermelon

Makes 300 ml (½ pint)

about 300 g (10 oz) **watermelon**

2 **oranges**, plus extra to serve (optional)

ice cubes

A great detoxing fruit, watermelon helps speed up the passage of toxin-carrying fluids through the system. This thirst-quenching juice is perfect on a hot summer's day.

1 Remove the skin and, if you want, the seeds from the watermelon and chop the flesh into chunks. Peel the oranges. Juice the watermelon and oranges.

2 Pour the juice into tall glasses over ice and serve immediately, decorated with slices of orange, if liked.

200 Kcals

iron

detox

Raspberry and watermelon

The red flesh of watermelon is a clue to the fact that it is a good source of lycopene, which is believed to reduce the risk of several cancers. The seeds are full of juice and can be juiced too.

1 Remove the skin and, if you want, the seeds from the watermelon and chop the flesh into chunks. Juice the raspberries with the melon.

2 Pour the juice into a tall glass, add a couple of ice cubes and serve immediately, decorated with raspberries, if liked.

Makes 350 ml (12 fl oz)

about 300 g (10 oz) **watermelon**

125 g (4 oz) **raspberries**, plus extra to serve (optional)

ice cubes

125
Kcals

iron

cleanse

Carrot

and apple

Makes 300 ml (½ pint)

4 **carrots**

2 green **apples**, plus extra to serve (optional)

ice cubes

Simply delicious, this juice is one of the best general tonics for internal cleansing and boosting your immune system. Both apples and carrots are exceptionally high in minerals and vitamins and are great cleansers.

1 Scrub the carrots. Chop the carrots and apples into evenly sized pieces and juice.

2 Pour the juice into tall glasses over ice and serve immediately, garnished with slices of apple, if liked.

280 Kcals

vit A

boost

Mixed berry fizz

This juice is low in calories but a useful source of calcium and vitamin C. The berries will help boost your immune system and, best of all, you won't even notice how healthy this fizzy drink is.

1 Freeze the berries for at least 2 hours or overnight. Juice the frozen berries.

2 Mix the juice with the sparkling water, pour into a tall glass over ice and serve immediately.

Makes 200 ml (7 fl oz)

150 g (5 oz)
mixed berries

100 ml (3½ fl oz)
sparkling **mineral water**

ice cubes

37
Kcals

vit C

revive

Red cabbage
and orange

Makes 200 ml (7 fl oz)

150 g (5 oz) **red cabbage**

50 g (2 oz) **orange**, plus
extra to serve (optional)

50 g (2 oz) **red grapes**

ice cubes

This juice can help protect against damage by free
radicals, thanks to its high content of antioxidant
vitamins A, C and E. The vivid colour of red
cabbage is caused by potent antioxidants that help
to prevent serious diseases.

1 Separate the cabbage into leaves. Peel the orange
and separate the flesh into segments. Juice the
grapes with the cabbage and orange.

2 Transfer the juice to a blender, add a couple of ice
cubes and process briefly.

3 Pour the juice into a glass and serve
immediately, decorated with a slice of orange,
if liked.

64
Kcals

vit A

satisfy

Broccoli and lettuce

If you feel a cold coming on or if your body's defences are going down, have a glass of this vitamin C- and calcium-rich juice. It is green power in a glass.

1 Separate the lettuce into leaves. Trim the celery and chop it into 5 cm (2 inch) pieces. Trim the broccoli and juice it with the lettuce and celery.

2 Pour the juice into a tall glass over ice and serve immediately. Alternatively, transfer it to a blender and process briefly with a couple of ice cubes for a smoother, creamier drink.

Makes 250 ml (8 fl oz)

100 g (3½ oz) **lettuce**
100 g (3½ oz) **celery**
150 g (5 oz) **broccoli**
ice cubes

70 Kcals

vit C

boost

Tomato and celery

Makes 200 ml (7 fl oz)

200 g (7 oz) **celery**

200 g (7 oz) **tomatoes**

celery salt

pepper

Tabasco sauce, to taste

ice cubes (optional)

This is an extremely healthy, low-carb juice, which is based on a non-alcoholic version of a Bloody Mary.

1 Trim the celery and cut it into 5 cm (2 inch) lengths. Juice the tomatoes with the celery.

2 Season the juice to taste with celery salt, pepper and Tabasco sauce.

3 Pour the juice into a tall glass over ice and serve immediately, or serve at room temperature without ice.

48 Kcals

calcium

appetize

Carrot
and lettuce

Carrots are probably the best vegetable source of carotenoids. This juice combines them with lettuce, so you can benefit from their high nutrient content.

1 Scrub the carrots and cut them into chunks. Separate the lettuce into leaves and juice them with the carrot.

2 Pour the juice into a tall glass over ice and serve immediately, garnished with chopped coriander.

Makes 200 ml (7 fl oz)

100 g (3½ oz) **carrots**

200 g (7 oz) **lettuce**

ice cubes

chopped fresh **coriander leaves**, to serve

63
Kcals

vit A

refresh

Carrot and celeriac

Makes 200 ml (7 fl oz)

100 g (3½ oz) **carrots**

100 g (3½ oz) **celeriac**

100 g (3½ oz) **celery**

ice cubes

1 **celery stick**, to serve (optional)

This is a classic vegetable combination. Carrots are vital for the immune system and are believed to protect against heart disease and some cancers. They also help regulate blood sugar levels and reduce blood cholesterol levels.

1 Scrub the carrots and peel the celeriac. Cut both into evenly sized chunks. Trim the celery and cut it into 5 cm (2 inch) lengths. Juice the vegetables.

2 Pour the juice into a tall glass over ice and serve immediately with a short celery stick, if liked.

55 Kcals

calcium

revitalize

Cucumber
and kiwifruit

Served over ice with lemon, this juice has a refreshing clean taste and will revive you when you are feeling sluggish and dehydrated.

1 Peel the cucumber and cut it into chunks. Peel the kiwifruit and juice it with the cucumber.

2 Pour the juice into a tall glass over ice and serve immediately. Alternatively, transfer it to a blender and process briefly with a couple of ice cubes for a smoother, creamier drink.

Makes 200 ml (7 fl oz)

200 g (7 oz) **cucumber**
100 g (3½ oz) **kiwifruit**
ice cubes (optional)

69
Kcals

vit C

revive

Cabbage and apple

Makes 200 ml (7 fl oz)

200 g (7 oz) **cabbage**

50 g (2 oz) **apple**

ice cubes

pinch of **ground cinnamon**, plus extra to serve

This tasty combination of flavours is a good way to enjoy cabbage juice. Cabbage is thought to fight cancer, particularly cancer of the colon, and it is also an excellent source of vitamins A, C and E.

1 Separate the cabbage into leaves and cut the apple into pieces. Juice the cabbage with the apple.

2 Transfer the juice to a blender, add a couple of ice cubes and a pinch of cinnamon and process briefly.

3 Pour the juice into a tall glass and serve immediately, with a sprinkling of cinnamon.

76 Kcals

vit E

boost

Apple and blackcurrant

Apples are naturally cleansing so they are great for your digestive system, especially if you have recently overindulged. If you process the juice in a blender with a couple of prunes, it can also alleviate constipation.

1 Chop the apples into chunks and juice them with the blackcurrants.

2 Pour the juice into a tall glass over ice and serve immediately, decorated with extra blackcurrants.

Makes 200 ml (7 fl oz)

300 g (10 oz) **apple**

200 g (7 oz) **blackcurrants**, plus extra to serve

ice cubes

30 Kcals

vit C

refresh

Celery and spinach

Makes 250 ml (8 fl oz)

100 g (3½ oz) **celery**

150 g (5 oz) **celeriac**

100 g (3½ oz) **lettuce**

100 g (3½ oz) **spinach**

ice cubes

This bright green juice makes an effective weekly detoxifying tonic. Like most green vegetable juices, blending it with ice will make it more creamy and palatable.

1 Trim the celery and cut it into 5 cm (2 inch) lengths. Peel and chop the celeriac into chunks. Separate the lettuce into leaves. Juice the spinach with the celery, celeriac and lettuce alternating the ingredients to make sure that the machine doesn't get clogged up with the leaves.

2 Transfer the juice to a blender, add a couple of ice cubes and process briefly. Serve immediately.

73 Kcals

calcium

detox

Orange and strawberry

This deliciously refreshing juice has a high vitamin C content to help ward off colds. Strawberries are natural painkillers and oranges are full of potassium, which is vital for rehydration.

1 Hull the strawberries. Peel the oranges and divide the flesh into segments. Juice the strawberries with the oranges.

2 Pour the juice into a tall glass over ice and serve immediately, decorated with sliced strawberries, if liked. Alternatively, transfer to a blender, add a couple of ice cubes and process briefly for a smoother, creamier drink.

Makes 200 ml (7 fl oz)

200 g (7 oz) **strawberries**, plus extra to serve (optional)

2 **oranges**

ice cubes

154 Kcals

vit C

sooth

Celery and fennel

Makes 200 ml (7 fl oz)

100 g (3½ oz) **celery**

100 g (3½ oz) **fennel**

75 g (3 oz) **pineapple**

ice cubes

As well as a useful amount of calcium, this juice contains plenty of vitamin C. Fennel also has appetite-controlling properties, which may help if you are trying to lose weight.

1 Trim the celery and cut it in 5 cm (2 inch) lengths. Cut the fennel into chunks. Peel the pineapple and remove the tough core. Juice the pineapple with the celery and fennel.

2 Pour the juice into a tall glass over ice and serve immediately.

49 Kcals

calcium

cleanse

Broccoli
and kale

This extra-green juice contains the superfood broccoli and can help to maintain your energy levels. It's also quite filling, so it's great for satisfying nagging hunger pangs.

1 Trim the broccoli and kale and juice them with the parsley, apple and celery.

2 Pour the juice into a tall glass over ice and serve immediately, garnished with kale, if liked.

Makes 200 ml (7 fl oz)

100 g (3½ oz) **broccoli**

100 g (3½ oz) **kale**, plus extra to serve (optional)

25 g (1 oz) **parsley**

200 g (7 oz) **apple**

50 g (2 oz) **celery**

ice cubes

228
Kcals

vit C

satisfy

Tomato and red pepper

Makes 200 ml (7 fl oz)

100 g (3½ oz)
red pepper

50 g (2 oz) **carrots**, plus ribbons to serve

100 g (3½ oz) **tomatoes**

ice cubes

This delicious drink is full of antioxidants. It tastes almost savoury, so you could try serving it as a starter at your next dinner party!

1 Core and deseed the pepper and roughly chop the flesh. Scrub the carrots and cut them into chunks. Juice the tomatoes with the pepper and carrots.

2 Pour the juice into a tall glass over ice and serve immediately, garnished with carrot ribbons.

66 Kcals

calcium

cleanse

Grapefruit and cucumber

This is a perfect choice if you don't fancy drinking alcohol. The cucumber flushes out the kidneys and the grapefruit aids the elimination of toxins. It is also a reviving juice for after exercise.

1 Cut the grapefruit in half and chop up the cucumber. Juice the lemon with the grapefruit and cucumber.

2 Pour the juice into tall glasses over ice and top up with mineral water. Serve immediately, decorated with chopped mint and slices of cucumber and lemon, if liked.

Makes 400 ml (14 fl oz)

625 g (1¼ lb) **grapefruit**

750 g (1½ lb) **cucumber**, plus extra to serve (optional)

1 **lemon**, plus extra to serve (optional)

ice cubes

sparkling **mineral water**

chopped **mint**, to serve

302 Kcals

vit C

revive

Broccoli
and parsnip

Makes 200 ml (7 fl oz)

50 g (2 oz) **parsnip**

50 g (2 oz) **apple**

150 g (5 oz) **broccoli**

ice cubes

This rich, rather sweet juice is bursting with vitamin C. Broccoli is believed to protect against heart disease and a range of infections. It stimulates the liver, which makes the whole body function better, and it is a good source of folic acid.

1 Scrub the parsnip and cut it into chunks. Chop the apple into quarters. Trim the broccoli and juice it with the parsnip and apple.

2 Transfer the juice to a blender, add a couple of ice cubes and process briefly. Serve immediately.

104 Kcals

vit C

revive

Ginger

and fennel

This warming drink tastes slightly spicy with the addition of ginger. Packed full of vitamins and antioxidents, this juice has excellent health-boosting properties.

1 Scrub and chop the carrots. Peel and roughly chop the ginger. Juice the fennel and celery with the carrots, ginger and spirulina (if used).

2 Pour the juice into a tall glass over ice and serve immediately, garnished with strips of fennel and fennel fronds, if liked.

Makes 200 ml (7 fl oz)

300 g (10 oz) **carrots**

2.5 cm (1 inch) cube **fresh root ginger**

50 g (2 oz) **fennel**, plus extra and fronds to serve (optional)

75 g (3 oz) **celery**

1 tablespoon **spirulina** (optional)

ice cubes

183 Kcals

vit A

energize

Spinach and lettuce

Makes 200 ml (7 fl oz)

175 g (6 oz) **carrots**

75 g (3 oz) **celery**

100 g (3½ oz) **spinach**

100 g (3½ oz) **lettuce**

25 g (1 oz) **parsley**, plus
extra to serve (optional)

ice cubes

This juice will prevent the build-up of toxins in
your system, which leads to sluggish metabolism
and low energy levels. Carrots, lettuce and celery
all work to regenerate the liver and lymph system
and aid digestion.

1 Scrub the carrots. Trim and chop the celery
into 5 cm (2 inch) lengths. Juice the spinach and
lettuce with the carrots and celery, alternating the
ingredients to make sure that the machine doesn't
get clogged up with the leaves.

2 Transfer the juice to a blender and process
briefly with a couple of ice cubes.

3 Pour the juice into a tall glass and serve
immediately, garnished with sprigs of parsley,
if liked.

137 Kcals

iron

detox

Cherry and cranberry

This juice will be particularly appreciated by anyone who likes a sour-tasting drink. Like other berries, cherries are an excellent source of antioxidants.

1 Pit the cherries and juice them together with the cranberries.

2 Mix the juice with the mineral water, pour it into a tall glass over ice and serve immediately.

Makes 200 ml (7 fl oz)

75 g (3 oz) **cherries**

75 g (3 oz) **cranberries**

100 ml (3½ fl oz) sparkling **mineral water**

ice cubes

47 Kcals

calcium

energize

Pear, celery and ginger

Makes 200 ml (7 fl oz)

100 g (3½ oz) **pear**

50 g (2 oz) **celery**

2.5 cm (1 inch) cube
fresh root ginger

ice cubes

Pears are a gentle, natural laxative, celery is a diuretic, and ginger promotes good digestion, making this a great juice for keeping your system balanced and regular.

1 Wash the pear. Trim the celery and cut it into 5 cm (2 inch) lengths. Peel and roughly chop the ginger. Juice the pear, celery and ginger.

2 Pour the juice into a tall glass over ice. Alternatively, transfer it to a blender and process briefly with a couple of ice cubes for a smoother, creamier drink.

50 Kcals

calcium

soothe

Cabbage
and pear

If you want to give your system a detox, this is the perfect juice. Cabbage aids digestion and prevents fluid retention. Celery, watercress and pear are the ideal accompaniments as they also contribute to the detoxification process.

1 Wash the pear and roughly chop the cabbage. Trim the celery and chop it into 5 cm (2 inch) lengths. Juice the watercress with the pear, cabbage and celery.

2 Pour the juice into a tall glass over ice and serve immediately with a short celery stick, if liked.

Makes 200 ml (7 fl oz)

250 g (8 oz) **pear**

125 g (4 oz) **cabbage**

50 g (2 oz) **celery**

25 g (1 oz) **watercress**

ice cubes

1 **celery stick**, to serve (optional)

206 Kcals

vit K

cleanse

Blackberry
and celeriac

Makes 200 ml (7 fl oz)

100 g (3½ oz)
blackberries, plus extra
to serve

100 g (3½ oz) **celeriac**

50 g (2 oz) **apple**

ice cubes

This juice will remind you of old-fashioned blackberry and apple pie. Blackberries can neutralize excessive acid, helping to relieve any aches and pains.

1 Freeze all the blackberries for at least 2 hours or overnight.

2 Peel the celeriac and cut it into chunks. Cut the apple into pieces and juice with the celeriac.

3 Transfer the juice to a blender, add the frozen blackberries and a couple of ice cubes and process it all briefly.

4 Pour the juice into a tall glass and serve immediately, decorated with frozen blackberries.

66 Kcals

calcium

satisfy

Strawberry and watermelon

Watermelon juice is so delicious that it's easy to drink a glass every day, and, by adding strawberries, you get a great boost of vitamin C as well as helping your body fight against harmful bacteria in your system.

1 Remove the skin and, if you want, the seeds from the watermelon and chop the flesh into chunks. Hull the strawberries. Juice the fruit.

2 Transfer the juice to a blender with a couple of ice cubes and process briefly.

3 Pour the juice into a tall glass and serve immediately, decorated with mint leaves and whole or sliced strawberries, if liked.

Makes 200 ml (7 fl oz)

200 g (7 oz) **watermelon**

200 g (7 oz) **strawberries**, plus extra to serve (optional)

ice cubes

mint leaves, to serve (optional)

130 Kcals

vit C

cleanse

Orange and passion fruit

Makes 200 ml (7 fl oz)

100 g (3½ oz) **orange**

1 **passion fruit**

100 ml (3½ fl oz)
sparkling **mineral water**

ice cubes

As well as being a great source of vitamin C, carotenoids and bioflavanoids, all of which are believed to help fight cancer, this juice is also a valuable source of calcium.

1 Peel the orange, segment the flesh and juice it.

2 Scoop the flesh out of the passion fruit and press the pulp through a tea strainer to extract the juice.

3 Mix the orange juice with the passion fruit juice and sparkling water and pour into a tall glass over ice. Serve immediately.

55 Kcals

vit C

boost

Spinach, celery and cucumber

This lovely green juice is a great all-round energy booster and the spinach will help strengthen your immune system. What more could you ask for?

1 Scrub the carrots and juice them with the other vegetables. Season the juice to taste with salt and pepper.

2 Pour the juice into a tall glass and serve garnished with tomato quarters, if liked.

Makes 200 ml (7 fl oz)

75 g (3 oz) **carrots**

50 g (2 oz) **green pepper**

25 g (1 oz) **spinach**

25 g (1 oz) **onion**

50 g (2 oz) **celery**

75 g (3 oz) **cucumber**

50 g (2 oz) **tomatoes**, plus extra to serve (optional)

salt and **pepper**

115 Kcals

vit E

energize

Pineapple
and alfalfa

Makes 250 ml (8 fl oz)

150 g (5 oz) **pineapple**

150 g (5 oz)
alfalfa sprouts

2–3 **ice cubes**

50 ml (2 fl oz) **water**

Pineapples are anti-inflammatory, antiviral and antibacterial, making them a superb addition to a healthy diet. The sweetness of the pineapple counteracts the rather bitter flavour of the alfalfa sprouts.

1 Peel the pineapple, remove the hard core and cut the flesh into chunks. Juice the pineapple.

2 Transfer the juice to a blender, add the alfalfa sprouts, ice cubes and water and process briefly.

3 Pour the juice into a tall glass and serve immediately.

97
Kcals

calcium

revive

92 juices

Apple
and avocado

This juice contains nutrient-dense avocados, which are rich in healthy monounsaturated fat, combined with vitamin C-packed kiwifruit and the cleansing properties of apple.

1 Quarter the apples. Trim the celery and chop it into 5 cm (2 inch) lengths. Juice the kiwifruit (there is no need to peel it) and lemon with the apples and celery.

2 Peel the avocado and remove the stone. Put the flesh in a blender, add the juice and process briefly.

3 Pour the juice into a tall glass and serve immediately, decorated with slices of kiwifruit, if liked.

Makes 200 ml (7 fl oz)

250 g (8 oz) **apple**

50 g (2 oz) **celery**

50 g (2 oz) **kiwifruit**, plus extra to serve (optional)

½ **lemon**

100 g (3½ oz) **avocado**

347 Kcals

vit C

satisfy

Kiwifruit
and lettuce

Makes 200 ml (7 fl oz)

100 g (3½ oz) **kiwifruit**, plus extra to serve (optional)

200 g (7 oz) **lettuce**

ice cubes

This a useful juice for anyone who may benefit from extra supplies of vitamin C. Lettuce adds its calming and soothing properties.

1 Peel the kiwifruit and roughly chop the flesh. Separate the lettuce into leaves. Juice the kiwifruit and lettuce.

2 Pour the juice into a tall glass over ice and serve immediately, decorated with slices of kiwifruit, if liked.

77
Kcals

vit C

boost

Radish
and carrot

Radish juice is too strong to be taken alone, but combined with carrot it has a soothing effect.

1 Scrub the carrots. Peel and roughly chop the ginger (if used). Juice the radishes with the carrots and ginger.

2 Pour the juice into a tall glass over ice and serve.

Makes 200 ml (7 fl oz)

175 g (6 oz) **carrots**

2.5 cm (1 inch) cube **fresh root ginger** (optional)

100 g (3½ oz) **radishes**, with tops and leaves

ice cubes

140
Kcals

zinc

cleanse

Raspberry
and celeriac

Makes 250 ml (8 fl oz)

150 g (5 oz) **raspberries**

150 g (5 oz) **celeriac**

ice cubes

Try this sharp and refreshing juice which is full of anti-inflammatory compounds and works as a natural aspirin.

1 Freeze the raspberries for at least 2 hours or overnight.

2 Peel the celeriac and cut it into chunks and juice it.

3 Transfer the juice to a blender, add the frozen raspberries and a couple of ice cubes and process it all briefly.

4 Pour the juice into a glass and serve immediately.

64 Kcals

calcium

refresh

Grapefruit
and kiwifruit

This clean-tasting drink is full of vitamins A and C, selenium and zinc. The best antioxidants are found in citrus fruit, strawberries, kiwifruit, raspberries and blueberries.

1 Remove the skin and tough core from the pineapple. Juice the grapefruit and kiwifruit (there is no need to peel it) with the pineapple.

2 Transfer the juice to a blender and process it briefly with the frozen berries.

3 Pour into a tall glass and serve immediately, decorated with raspberries, if liked.

Makes 200 ml (7 fl oz)

175 g (6 oz) **pineapple**

150 g (5 oz) **grapefruit**

50 g (2 oz) **kiwifruit**

50 g (2 oz) frozen **raspberries**, plus extra to serve (optional)

50 g (2 oz) frozen **cranberries**

247
Kcals

vit A

revive

Pineapple
and lettuce

Makes 200 ml (7 fl oz)

75 g (3 oz) **pineapple**, peeled and cored

200 g (7 oz) **lettuce**

ice cubes

mint leaves, to serve

This juice is an ideal way to top up your energy levels. Pineapple should always be combined with a more neutral ingredient, such as lettuce, because it is high in acids that can damage tooth enamel if taken in excess.

1 Peel and core the pineapple and chop the flesh into chunks. Separate the lettuce into leaves. Juice the pineapple and lettuce.

2 Pour into a tall glass over ice and serve immediately, decorated with mint leaves. Alternatively, put the pineapple and lettuce into a blender with a couple of ice cubes and a few mint leaves and process briefly for a smoother, creamier drink.

58 Kcals

calcium

energize

Broccoli
and beetroot

Beetroot gives juices an intense red-purple colour and the globes also contain high levels of antioxidants and vitamins.

1 Scrub the carrots and beetroot. Trim the broccoli. Juice the vegetables.

2 Pour the juice into a tall glass and serve garnished with a sprig of coriander, if liked.

Makes 200 ml (7 fl oz)

175 g (6 oz) **carrots**

50 g (2 oz) **beetroot**

250 g (8 oz) **broccoli**

sprig of fresh **coriander**, to serve (optional)

172 Kcals

vit A

boost

Cranberry and apple

Makes 200 ml (7 fl oz)

50 g (2 oz) **apple**

100 g (3½ oz) **lettuce**

50 g (2 oz) **cranberries**

ice cubes

Apples are an excellent base for juices as they blend well with almost all other ingredients. They are also good for cleansing the digestive tract and are a good source of vitamin C.

1 Cut the apple into slices. Separate the lettuce into leaves. Juice the cranberries together with the apple and lettuce.

2 Transfer the juice to a blender, add a couple of ice cubes and process briefly. Serve immediately.

61 Kcals

vit C

cleanse

Mango and strawberry

This delicious, vivid red juice is bursting with beta-carotene, making it ideal for boosting your immune system, the body's defence against disease.

1 Remove the skin and, if you want, the seeds from the watermelon and chop the flesh into chunks. Hull the strawberries and peel the mango and remove the stone. Juice the fruit with the pepper and tomatoes.

2 Transfer the juice to a blender, add a couple of ice cubes and process briefly.

3 Pour the juice into a tall glass and serve immediately, decorated with mango slices, if liked.

Makes 200 ml (7 fl oz)

125 g (4 oz) **watermelon**

125 g (4 oz) **strawberries**

125 g (4 oz) **mango**, plus extra to serve (optional)

100 g (3½ oz) **red pepper**

50 g (2 oz) **tomatoes**

ice cubes

200 Kcals

vit A

boost

Grapefruit
and lettuce

Makes 200 ml (7 fl oz)

75 g (3 oz) **grapefruit**

125 g (4 oz) **lettuce**

75 g (3 oz) **celery**, trimmed

50 g (2 oz) **pear**

ice cubes

In this juice the pear provides a hint of natural sweetness, which is nicely counterbalanced by the tangy grapefruit, celery and lettuce.

1 Peel and segment the grapefruit. Separate the lettuce into leaves. Cut the celery into 5 cm (2 inch) lengths. Wash and quarter the pear. Juice the fruit with the lettuce and celery.

2 Pour the juice into a tall glass over ice and serve immediately.

71 Kcals

calcium

refresh

Ginger
and melon

This juice rich in antioxidants, and the lime encourages the elimination of toxins from the body. Ginger has been used for centuries as an aid to digestion and as a popular remedy for nausea.

1 Scrub the carrots and peel and roughly chop the ginger. Remove the skin and seeds from the melon and chop the flesh into chunks. Juice the lime with the carrots, ginger and melon.

2 Pour the juice into a tall glass over ice and serve immediately, decorated with lime wedges and seeds from a cardamom pod, if liked.

Makes 200 ml (7 fl oz)

125 g (4 oz) **carrots**

2.5 cm (1 inch) cube **fresh root ginger**

250 g (8 oz) **cantaloupe melon**

1 **lime**, plus extra to serve

ice cubes

cardamom, to serve (optional)

166 Kcals

vit A

detox

Orange
and alfalfa

Makes 200 ml (7 fl oz)

100 g (3½ oz) **orange**,
plus extra to serve
(optional)

100 g (3½ oz) **celeriac**

100 g (3½ oz)
alfalfa sprouts

Combining orange with celeriac and alfalfa sprouts
gives you a juice with a zingy flavour that is also
packed with healthy enzymes. Celeriac, which has
a taste similar to celery, contains good levels of
vitamin C.

1 Peel the orange and separate it into segments.
Peel the celeriac and cut it into chunks. Rinse the
alfalfa sprouts. Juice all the ingredients.

2 Pour the juice into a tall glass and serve
immediately, decorated with extra slices of orange,
if liked.

79 Kcals

calcium

boost

Peach
and ginger

This sparkling drink is not only delicious, but it can also help to calm an upset stomach or ease morning sickness. Peach has an alkalizing effect on the digestive system, and ginger works wonders for nausea.

1 Halve the peaches and remove the stones. Peel and roughly chop the ginger. Juice the peaches and ginger.

2 Pour the juice into a tall glass over ice, add a splash of sparkling water and a couple of mint leaves and serve immediately.

Makes 200 ml (7 fl oz)

250 g (8 oz) **peaches**
2.5 cm (1 inch) cube **fresh root ginger**
ice cubes
sparkling **mineral water**
mint leaves

127
Kcals

vit A

soothe

Pineapple and celery

Makes 200 ml (7 fl oz)

125 g (4 oz) **pineapple**

125 g (4 oz) **lettuce**

125 g (4 oz) **celery**, trimmed

ice cubes

1 **celery stick**, to serve (optional)

This juice is detoxifying and calming, as lettuce is one of nature's tranquillizers. The darker the leaves, the more nutrients they contain, so cos (romaine) and red-leaved lettuces are far more health-boosting than the pale iceberg types.

1 Peel the pineapple, remove the tough core and chop the flesh into chunks. Separate the lettuce into leaves. Trim the celery and cut it into 5 cm (2 inch) lengths. Juice the pineapple together with the lettuce and celery.

2 Pour the juice into a tall glass over ice and serve immediately with a stick of celery, if liked.

77 Kcals

calcium

detox

Lettuce, parsnip and melon

This juice is rich in folic acid and vitamin A, making it an ideal choice for general health and especially if you're pregnant.

1 Scrub the carrots and parsnips. Separate the lettuce leaves. Remove the skin and seeds from the melon and chop the flesh into chunks. Juice the melon with the carrots, parsnip and lettuce, adding the ingredients alternately so that the leaves don't clog the machine.

2 Pour the juice into a tall glass and serve decorated with wedges of melon, if liked.

Makes 200 ml (7 fl oz)

125 g (4 oz) **carrots**

125 g (4 oz) **parsnips**

125 g (4 oz) **lettuce**

125 g (4 oz) **cantaloupe melon**, plus extra to serve (optional)

204 Kcals

folic acid

energize

Strawberry and tomato

Makes 200 ml (7 fl oz)

100 g (3½ oz) **strawberries**, hulled

200 g (7 oz) **tomatoes**

basil leaves

ice cubes

This colourful juice sounds like it has an unusual combination of ingredients, but they're full of phytonutrients, which have been shown to contain anti-cancer properties.

1 Hull the strawberries and juice them with the tomatoes and a few basil leaves, reserving a couple of leaves for decoration.

2 Pour the juice into a tall glass over ice and serve immediately, decorated with the reserved basil leaves.

61 Kcals

calcium

boost

Endive
and celery

The combination of vegetables in this juice means it is packed with vitamin A. The salad ingredients in this juice make it feel very virtuous to drink!

1 Scrub the carrots and cut the celery into 5 cm (2 inch) lengths. Juice the endive with the carrots and celery.

2 Transfer the juice to a blender, add a couple of ice cubes and process briefly.

3 Pour the juice into a tall glass and serve immediately, garnished with slices of lemon slices and some chopped parsley, if liked.

Makes 200 ml (7 fl oz)

175 g (6 oz) **carrots**

125 g (4 oz) **celery**

125 g (4 oz) **endive**

ice cubes

lemon slices, to serve

chopped **parsley**, to serve (optional)

128
Kcals

vit A

revive

Celery, ginger and pineapple

Makes 200 ml (7 fl oz)

125 g (4 oz) **celery**

125 g (4 oz) **pineapple**

2.5 cm (1 inch) cube
fresh root ginger

crushed ice

This juice is brilliant for your digestive system. Ginger can help relieve indigestion and and is also useful for treating coughs, colds and flu-like symptoms.

1 Trim the celery and cut it into 5 cm (2 inch) lengths. Peel the pineapple, remove the tough core and cut the flesh into chunks. Peel and roughly chop the ginger. Juice the celery with the pineapple and ginger.

2 Transfer the juice to a blender, add some crushed ice and process briefly. Serve immediately.

64 Kcals

calcium

refresh

Cabbage and red pepper

All four ingredients in this juice contain bioflavonoids, which reduce inflammation, making it very beneficial for the skin.

1 Juice together the pepper, tomatoes and cabbage.

2 Pour the juice into a tall glass, stir in the parsley and serve immediately, decorated with lime wedges, if liked.

Makes 200 ml (7 fl oz)

175 g (6 oz) **red pepper**

175 g (6 oz) **tomatoes**

100 g (3½ oz) **white cabbage**

1 tablespoon chopped **parsley**

lime wedges, to serve (optional)

120 Kcals

vit A

cleanse

Melon, berry and cherry

Makes 150 ml (¼ pint)

about 100 g (3½ oz) **watermelon**, plus extra to serve

50 g (2 oz) **cherries**

50 g (2 oz) **blackberries**

ice cubes

Drink a glass of this rich juice instead of wine. The melon is excellent for cleansing the system, and the cherries have a whole host of benefits.

1 Remove the skin and, if you want, the seeds from the melon and chop the flesh into chunks. Pit the cherries and hull the blackberries. Juice the fruit.

2 Pour the juice into a tall glass over ice and serve immediately, decorated with a slice of watermelon.

67 Kcals

calcium

soothe

Radish and potato

This vegetable juice contains potatoes which are really great for juicing and are a good source of vitamin C.

1 Scrub the potatoes and carrots. Juice the radishes and cucumber with the potatoes and carrots.

2 Transfer the juice to a blender, add a couple of ice cubes and process briefly.

3 Pour the juice into a tall glass and serve immediately, garnished with slices of radish, if liked.

Makes 200 ml (7 fl oz)

100 g (3½ oz) **potatoes**

100 g (3½ oz) **carrots**

100 g (3½ oz) **radishes**, plus extra to serve (optional)

100 g (3½ oz) **cucumber**

ice cubes

155 Kcals

vit C

detox

Red pepper and tomato

Makes 200 ml (7 fl oz)

50 g (2 oz) **red pepper**

50 g (2 oz) **cucumber**

30 g (1¼ oz)
spring onions

100 ml (3½ fl oz)
tomato juice

lemon juice

hot pepper sauce

Worcestershire sauce

salt and **pepper**

This lovely juice makes an ideal aperitif with a few olives and some nuts. As well as tasting so good, it's packed with vitamin C and calcium.

1 Core and deseed the pepper and roughly chop the flesh. Peel the cucumber. Roughly chop the spring onions, reserving a few shreds for garnish.

2 Pour the tomato juice into a blender, add the red pepper, cucumber and spring onions and process. Season to taste with lemon juice, hot pepper sauce, Worcestershire sauce, salt and pepper.

3 Pour the juice into a tall glass and serve immediately, garnished with the reserved shreds of spring onion.

40
Kcals

vit C

vitalize

Green pepper and parsnip

Like all root vegetables, parsnips are high in potassium, which helps to strengthen the roots of your hair. Enjoy this delicious juice and get a healthy head of hair.

1 Scrub the parsnips and cut into chunks. Juice the green pepper, watercress and cucumber with the parsnips.

2 Pour the juice into a tall glass over ice and serve immediately with a sprinkling of chopped mint.

Makes 200 ml (7 fl oz)

175 g (6 oz) **parsnips**

175 g (6 oz) **green pepper**

100 g (3½ oz) **watercress**

175 g (6 oz) **cucumber**

ice cubes

chopped **mint**, to serve

211
Kcals

vit A

boost

Grapefruit and cucumber

Makes 200 ml (7 fl oz)

200 g (7 oz) **cucumber**

100 ml (3½ fl oz) **grapefruit juice**

6 **ice cubes**

Served over ice, this is a cooling and very easy-to-make summertime juice that will cleanse and refresh your system.

1 Peel and roughly chop the cucumber and put it in a blender. Add the grapefruit juice and ice cubes and process until the ice is coarsely crushed.

2 Pour the juice into a tall glass and serve immediately.

26 Kcals

calcium

refresh

Grapefruit
and spinach

Anyone can enjoy this wonderful juice and it's made especially refreshing with the addition of the sharp grapefruit.

1 Peel the grapefruit, keeping as much of the pith as possible. Scrub the carrots. Juice the spinach with the grapefruit and carrots.

2 Pour the juice into a tall glass and serve decorated with slices of grapefruit, if liked.

Makes 200 ml (7 fl oz)

125 g (4 oz) **pink grapefruit**, plus extra to serve (optional)

125 g (4 oz) **carrots**

125 g (4 oz) **spinach**

185 Kcals

vit A

soothe

Turnip and broccoli

Makes 200 ml (7 fl oz)

125 g (4 oz) **turnips**, including the tops

125 g (4 oz) **carrots**

125 g (4 oz) **broccoli**

handful **dandelion leaves**, plus extra to serve (optional)

175 g (6 oz) **apple**

ice cubes

Turnip-top leaves contain more calcium than milk. Broccoli is also valuable because it contains good quantities of both calcium and folic acid. Dandelion leaves are an excellent source of magnesium.

1 Scrub the turnips and carrots. Juice the broccoli, dandelion leaves and apples with the root vegetables.

2 Transfer the juice to a blender, add a couple of ice cubes and process briefly.

3 Pour the juice into a tall glass and serve immediately, garnished with dandelion leaves, if liked.

196 Kcals

calcium

revive

Grape and plum

This fruity juice is a good source of potassium, vitamin E and iron. The rich flavour makes it ideal to drink in the evening after a meal.

1 Halve the plums, remove the stones and roughly chop the flesh. Juice the grapes with the plums.

2 Pour the juice into a tall glass over ice and serve immediately, decorated with slices of plum, if liked.

Makes 300 ml (½ pint)

about 300 g (10 oz) **plums**, plus extra to serve (optional)

150 g (5 oz) seedless **red grapes**

ice cubes

190 Kcals

niacin

boost

Papaya
and orange

Makes 200 ml (7 fl oz)

125 g (4 oz) **papaya**, plus extra to serve (optional)

2 **oranges**

125 g (4 oz) **cucumber**, plus extra to serve (optional)

ice cubes

The overall effect of this delicious juice is calming and rehydrating. Papaya helps to calm the digestive system, cucumber flushes out toxins and orange gives a great boost of vitamin C.

1 Peel the papaya and the oranges (leaving on as much pith as possible). Juice the cucumber with the papaya and oranges.

2 Pour the juice into a tall glass over ice and serve immediately, decorated with slices of cucumber and papaya, if liked.

184 Kcals

vit C

revive

Kiwifruit and black grape

This juice contains large amounts of carbohydrate, so it's superb for giving your body a real energy boost. Kiwifruit are an excellent source of vitamin C.

1 Peel the kiwifruit, chop the flesh into evenly sized pieces and juice them with the grapes.

2 Transfer the juice to a blender, add some crushed ice and process briefly.

2 Pour the juice into a tall glass and serve garnished with a twist of lemon and a sprig of mint.

Makes 300 ml (½ pint)

2 **kiwifruit**

300 g (10 oz) seedless **black grapes**

crushed ice

lemon twist

sprig of **mint**

240 Kcals

calcium

energize

Red cabbage
and carrot

Makes 200 ml (7 fl oz)

175 g (6 oz) **carrots**

250 g (8 oz) **apple**

125 g (4 oz) **red cabbage**, plus extra to serve (optional)

ice cubes

This juice is a healthy way to regulate your system and enjoy a delicious drink, all in one go.

1 Scrub the carrots. Juice the apples (including the pips) and cabbage with the carrots.

2 Pour the juice into a tall glass over ice and serve immediately, garnished with slivers of red cabbage, if liked.

250 Kcals

vit K

calm

Strawberry and peach

A deficiency in iron can make you feel tired and listless. This vitamin-rich juice also provides useful amounts of iron.

1 Wash and hull the strawberries. Cut the peaches in half, remove the stones and roughly chop the flesh. Cut the apple into chunks. Juice the fruit.

2 Add the juice to the water, pour it into 2 tall glasses and serve with a couple of ice cubes in each, if liked.

Makes 600 ml (1 pint)

125 g (4 oz) **strawberries**

2 **peaches**

1 red **apple**

300 ml (½ pint) **water**

ice cubes (optional), to serve

 153 Kcals

 iron

 boost

Prune and spinach

Makes 200 ml (7 fl oz)

25 g (1 oz) ready-to-eat **prunes**

250 g (8 oz) **pears**, plus extra to serve (optional)

125 g (4 oz) **spinach**

ice cubes

This juice is ideal if you are constipated, as prunes and spinach are both a natural laxative.

1 If necessary, remove the stones from the prunes. Juice the pears and spinach with the prunes.

2 Pour the juice into a tall glass over ice and serve immediately, decorated with slices of pear, if liked.

302 Kcals

vit A

detox

Orange, apple and pear

This juice is especially good for replenishing repleted energy stores. It is also a good source of calcium. The addition of honey gives an extra energy boost, which may be welcome.

1 Peel the oranges and divide the flesh into segments. Chop the apple and pear into evenly sized pieces. Juice the fruit.

2 Pour the juice into a tall glass, stir in the honey (if used), add a couple of ice cubes and serve.

Makes 350 ml (12 fl oz)

2 **oranges**

1 red **apple**

1 **pear**

1 teaspoon **clear honey** (optional)

ice cubes, to serve

218 Kcals

calcium

boost

Apple and blueberry

Makes 150 ml (¼ pint)

250 g (8 oz) **apple**

125 g (4 oz) fresh or frozen **blueberries**

This powerful infection-fighting juice contains blueberries, which are packed with antioxidants. They neutralize harmful free radicals in the body and help maintain a healthy heart.

1 Chop the apple into pieces (including the pips) and juice it.

2 Transfer the juice to a blender, add the blueberries and process. Serve immediately.

210 Kcals

vit E

soothe

Strawberry
and kiwifruit

Packed with vitamin C, this juice would be good during exercise, because vitamin C is thought to increase oxygen uptake and aerobic energy production. Perfect for the gym!

1 Hull the strawberries. Peel the kiwifruit and slice the flesh into evenly sized pieces. Juice the fruit.

2 Pour the juice into a tall glass, add a couple of ice cubes, if liked, and serve immediately.

Makes 300 ml (½ pint)

150 g (5 oz) **strawberries**

2 **kiwifruit**

ice cubes (optional)

100
Kcals

vit C

energize

Carrot and cabbage

Makes 200 ml (7 fl oz)

250 g (8 oz) **carrots**

250 g (8 oz) **cabbage**

ice cubes

This juice combines the power of carrots and cabbages, which are both renowned for having a healing effect on the stomach.

1 Scrub the carrots. Juice the cabbage and carrots.

2 Pour the juice into a tall glass over ice and serve immediately.

180
Kcals

vit K

heal

Grapefruit and pineapple

This is a delicious thirst-quencher in which the sweetness of the pineapple perfectly complements the tarter flavour of the grapefruit.

1 Peel the grapefruit and divide the flesh into segments. Remove the skin and hard central core from the pineapple and cut the flesh into chunks. Juice the fruit.

2 Mix the juice with the water, pour it into a glass, add a couple of ice cubes, if liked, and serve immediately.

Makes 600 ml (1 pint)

1 **pink grapefruit**

about 225 g (7½ oz) **pineapple**

300 ml (½ pint) **water**

ice cubes (optional)

140 Kcals

vit C

satisfy

Ginger
and apple

Makes 100 ml (3½ fl oz)

2.5 cm (1 inch) cube
fresh root ginger

250 g (8 oz) **apple**

ice cubes

chopped **mint**, to serve
(optional)

sparkling **mineral water**
(optional)

Drink this refreshing juice just before travelling.
Said to be more effective than anything you can get
over the pharmacy counter, ginger is ideal for
quelling nausea.

1 Peel and roughly chop the ginger. Juice the
apple with the ginger.

2 Pour the juice into a glass over ice and serve
immediately, decorate with chopped mint, if liked.
Alternatively, the juice can be diluted with
sparkling mineral water to taste.

 160 Kcals

 vit A

 calm

Orange and cranberry

Oranges, cranberries and mangoes are packed with the antioxidant vitamin C and the bonus is that they all taste delicious.

1 Wash the cranberries; if you are using frozen cranberries, thaw them first. Peel the mango and remove the stone. Peel the orange and divide the flesh into segments. Juice the fruit.

2 Pour the juice into a glass, stir in the water and honey, add a couple of ice cubes and serve immediately, decorated with cranberries, if liked.

Makes 400 ml (14 fl oz)

125 g (4 oz) **cranberries**, plus extra to serve (optional)

1 **mango**

1 **orange**

100 ml (3½ fl oz) **water**

1 teaspoon **clear honey**

ice cubes

183
Kcals

vit C

boost

Red onion and beetroot

Makes 200 ml (7 fl oz)

250 g (8 oz) **carrots**

125 g (4 oz) **beetroot**,
plus leaves to serve
(optional)

125 g (4 oz) **watercress**

125 g (4 oz) **red onion**

1 **garlic clove**

The ingredients in this juice pack a real flavour punch and are also great for the blood. The juice is an excellent source of vitamins A, B6, C and E.

1 Scrub the carrots and beetroot. Juice the watercress, onion and garlic with the carrots and beetroot.

2 Pour the juice into a tall glass and serve garnished with beet leaves, if liked.

167 Kcals

vit A

energize

Orange
and apricot

This juice contains plenty of calcium and iron.
Fresh apricots have a short season, so it's important
to make the most of them when they are available,
but if you can't get fresh apricots try peaches
or nectarines.

1 Halve the apricots and remove the stones. Peel
the orange and divide the flesh into segments. Juice
the fruit.

2 Mix the juice with the water, pour it into a tall
glass, add ice cubes, if liked, and serve immediately.

Makes 300 ml (½ pint)

150 g (5 oz) **apricots**
½ large **orange**
150 ml (¼ pint) **water**
ice cubes (optional)

75
Kcals

iron

boost

Pear and watercress

Makes 50 ml (2 fl oz)

250 g (8 oz) **pears**

125 g (4 oz) **watercress**

½ **lemon**, plus extra to serve (optional)

ice cubes

The distinctive, peppery taste of watercress makes it a popular garnish, but make the most of its health-boosting properties by adding it to juices.

1 Wash the pears and juice them with the watercress and lemon.

2 Pour the juice into a tall glass over ice, add a twist of lemon, if liked, and serve immediately.

172 Kcals

vit A

refresh

Orange and raspberry

This juice is a great choice if you are exercising or doing some other demanding activity, it will provide a good boost of vitamin C.

1 Peel the orange and divide the flesh into segments. Juice the raspberries with the orange.

2 Mix the juice with the water, pour into a tall glass over ice and serve immediately.

Makes 250 ml (8 fl oz)

1 large **orange**
75 g (3 oz) **raspberries**
125 ml (4 fl oz) **water**
ice cubes

77
Kcals

vit C

energize

Spinach and spirulina

Makes 200 ml (7 fl oz)

250 g (8 oz) **carrots**, plus
extra to serve (optional)

250 g (8 oz) **spinach**

25 g (1 oz) **parsley**

1 teaspoon **spirulina**

Drink this incredibly healthy juice if you lack iron
in your diet. It will help to prevent anaemia, which
can leave you feeling lethargic, depressed and
prone to colds.

1 Scrub the carrots. Juice the spinach and parsley
with the carrots.

2 Pour the juice into a tall glass, stir in the
spirulina and serve immediately, garnished with
slivers of carrot, if liked.

229
Kcals

iron

revive

Melon and kiwifruit

This juice is really high in nutrients, but not too heavy, so it's ideal to drink during activity. It contains good amounts of calcium and carbohydrate, while kiwifruit is rich in vitamin C.

1 Remove the skin and seeds from the melon and chop the flesh into chunks. Peel the kiwifruit and chop the flesh into pieces. Juice the grapes with the melon and kiwifruit.

2 Pour the juice into a tall glass over ice and serve immediately.

Makes 300 ml (½ pint)

375 g (12 oz) **honeydew melon**

2 **kiwifruit**

125 g (4 oz) seedless **green grapes**

ice cubes

232 Kcals

calcium

boost

Carrot and artichoke

Makes 200 ml (7 fl oz)

100 g (3½ oz) **carrots**, plus extra to serve (optional)

100 g (3½ oz) **Jerusalem artichokes**

100 g (3½ oz) **lettuce**

100 g (3½ oz) **Brussels sprouts**

100 g (3½ oz) **green beans**, plus extra to serve (optional)

½ **lemon**

Although this juice may not be to everyone's taste, Brussels sprouts are a top source of the antioxidants, especially vitamins A and C, that are useful for keeping the body disease free.

1 Scrub the carrots and Jerusalem artichokes. Separate the lettuce leaves. Juice the Brussels sprouts, beans and lemon with the carrots, artichokes and lettuce leaves.

2 Pour the juice into a tall glass and serve immediately, garnished with slivers of green beans and carrot, if liked.

186 Kcals

vit A

balance

Spinach and yellow pepper

This juice contains cinnamon, which is renowned for stabilizing blood sugar. To give the juice an extra boost, stir 1 tablespoon of raw wheatgerm into the finished juice.

1 Juice the spinach, apple and pepper.

2 Pour the juice into a tall glass, stir in the ground cinnamon and serve immediately, garnished with a cinnamon stick, if liked.

aMakes 200 ml (7 fl oz)

125 g (4 oz) **spinach**

250 g (8 oz) **apple**

100 g (3½ oz) **yellow pepper**

pinch of **ground cinnamon**

1 **cinnamon stick**, to serve (optional)

222 Kcals

vit C

energize

Kiwifruit and pomegranate

Makes 150 ml (¼ pint)

250 g (8 oz) **kiwifruit**

125 g (4 oz) **cucumber**

1 tablespoon
pomegranate seeds
(optional)

lime, to serve (optional)

Studies have suggested that the antioxidant action of pomegranate juice is three times more potent than a similar quantity of red wine or green tea.

1 Wash the kiwifruit and cucumber but don't peel them because both contain nutrients in their skins. Juice them.

2 Pour the juice into a tall glass, stir in the pomegranate seeds (if used) and serve immediately, decorated with a slice of lime, if liked.

168 Kcals

vit C

calm

Blueberry and grapefruit

You get a double hit of goodness in this juice.
Grapefruit is particularly recommended as a rich
source of vitamin C and blueberries are also
extremely potent antioxidants.

1 Peel and roughly chop the ginger. Juice the
blueberries, grapefruit and apple with the ginger.

2 Pour the juice into a tall glass over ice and serve
immediately, decorated with thin slices of ginger,
if liked.

Makes 200 ml (7 fl oz)

2.5 cm (1 inch) cube
fresh root ginger, plus
extra to serve (optional)

250 g (8 oz) **blueberries**

125 g (4 oz) **grapefruit**

250 g (8 oz) **apple**

ice cubes

380
Kcals

vit C

energize

Lettuce
and fennel

Makes 150 ml (¼ pint)

175 g (6 oz) **lettuce**, plus extra to serve (optional)

125 g (4 oz) **fennel**

½ **lemon**, plus extra to serve (optional)

ice cubes

The combination of lettuce and fennel make this an extremely calming juice.

1 Separate the lettuce leaves. Juice the fennel and lemon with the lettuce.

2 Pour the juice into a tall glass over ice and serve immediately, garnished with lemon slivers and lettuce leaves, if liked.

 72 Kcals

 vit C

 soothe

Apple and blackberry

Blackberries are rich in the antioxidant vitamins C and E, and this juice provides an excellent amount of vitamin E as well as some iron and calcium. Choose a sweet apple, such as Braeburn or Pink Lady, because blackberries can be tart.

1 Cut the apples into chunks. Juice the blackberries with the apples.

2 Pour the juice into a glass, stir in the water, add a couple of ice cubes and serve immediately.

Makes 300 ml (½ pint)

1½ **apples**
75 g (3 oz) **blackberries**
150 ml (¼ pint) **water**
ice cubes

90
Kcals

vit E

boost

Apple and plum

Makes 300 ml (½ pint)

about 300 g (10 oz) ripe dessert **plums**

3 red **apples**

ice cubes

If you choose plums that are ripe but not overripe, you will find it easier to remove the stones before juicing them.

1 Cut the plums into quarters and remove the stones. Cut the apples into evenly sized pieces. Juice the fruit.

2 Pour the juice into a tall glass over ice and serve immediately.

210 Kcals

calcium

revive

Kale and spirulina

This juice is a great energy booster with nutritional benefits that far outweigh its flavour.

1 Juice the kale and the wheatgrass.

2 Pour the juice into a small glass, stir in the spirulina powder and serve garnished with wheatgrass blades.

Makes 50 ml (2 fl oz)

25 g (1 oz) **kale**

100 g (3½ oz) **wheatgrass**, plus extra to serve

1 teaspoon **spirulina**

30 Kcals

calcium

boost

Strawberry and beetroot

Makes 200 ml (7 fl oz)

250 g (8 oz) **carrots**

125 g (4 oz) **beetroot**

1 **orange**

125 g (4 oz) **strawberries**, plus extra to serve

2–3 **ice cubes**

Fight lethargy with this energy-boosting juice. Carrots are great for the immune system and reduce blood cholesterol levels.

1 Scrub the carrots and beetroot. Juice the orange with the carrots and beetroot.

2 Hull the strawberries. Transfer the juice to a blender, add the strawberries and a couple of ice cubes and process briefly.

3 Pour the juice into a tall glass and serve immediately, decorated with a strawberry.

259 Kcals

vit A

energize

Celery, fennel and lettuce

Celery and fennel help the body utilize magnesium and calcium to calm the nerves. Coupling these vegetables with the sedative effect of lettuce makes this juice an ideal stress buster.

1 Trim the celery and cut it into 5 cm (2 inch) lengths. Separate the lettuce leaves. Remove the skin and tough core of the pineapple. Juice the fennel with the celery, lettuce and pineapple.

2 Transfer the juice to a blender, add the tarragon and a couple of ice cubes and process briefly.

3 Pour the juice into a tall glass and serve immediately, decorated with tarragon sprigs, if liked.

Makes 200 ml (7 fl oz)

50 g (2 oz) **celery**

125 g (4 oz) cos (romaine) **lettuce**

175 g (6 oz) **pineapple**

50 g (2 oz) **fennel**

1 teaspoon chopped **tarragon**, plus sprigs to serve (optional)

ice cubes

128 Kcals

calcium

soothe

Peppers and orange

Makes 200 ml (7 fl oz)

100 g (3½ oz)
red pepper

100 g (3½ oz)
yellow pepper

100 g (3½ oz)
orange pepper

1 **orange**

1 tablespoon **mint leaves**, plus extra to serve (optional)

ice cubes

Peppers are a favourite for warding off infection, and are also natural painkillers. This juice is a good choice if you are run down and fighting the winter round of colds and flu.

1 Juice the peppers with the orange.

2 Pour the juice into a tall glass over ice, stir in the mint and serve immediately, decorated with mint leaves, if liked.

 141 Kcals

 vit C

 boost

Spinach, carrot and tomato

If you are very active, this juice is a good choice as it's full of iron, vitamins and folic acid.

1 Wash and drain the spinach. Scrub the carrots. Juice the tomatoes and pepper with the spinach and carrots, alternating the vegetables to make sure that the machine doesn't get clogged up with the leaves.

2 Pour the juice into a tall glass over ice and serve immediately.

Makes 300 ml (½ pint)

large handful
baby **spinach**

200 g (7 oz) **carrots**

4 **tomatoes**

½ **red pepper**

ice cubes

175
Kcals

iron

revive

Papaya and grapefruit

Makes 200 ml (7 fl oz)

150 g (5 oz) **papaya**

150 g (5 oz) **grapefruit**

150 g (5 oz) **raspberries**

juice of ½ **lime**, plus slices to serve (optional)

ice cubes

This sweet juice is a potent cocktail of vitamins. Containing more vitamin C and potassium than oranges, papayas are nutritional superfoods.

1 Scoop out the flesh of the papaya. Peel the grapefruit, leaving on as much pith as possible. Juice the raspberries together with the papaya and grapefruit.

2 Pour the juice into a tall glass over ice, stir in the lime juice and serve immediately, decorated with slices of lime, if liked.

193 Kcals

vit C

boost

Carrot and grapefruit

Pink grapefruits are a good source of folic acid. They also contain the antioxidant lycopene, which is believed to protect the body against some cancers and heart disease. Pink grapefruits are sweeter than the yellow variety, making this juice a little more palatable.

1 Scrub the carrot. Peel the grapefruit and divide into segments. Juice the apple with the carrot and grapefruit, then add the water.

2 Pour the juice into tall glasses over ice and serve immediately, decorated with slices of apple, if liked.

Makes 375 ml (13 fl oz)

1 **carrot**

½ **pink grapefruit**

1 **apple**, plus extra to serve (optional)

200 ml (7 fl oz) **water**

ice cubes

210 Kcals

folic acid

energize

Chilli and pineapple

Makes 200 ml (7 fl oz)

250 g (8 oz) **carrots**

½ small **chilli**
or a sprinkling of
chilli powder

250 g (8 oz) **pineapple**

ice cubes

juice of ½ **lime**

1 tablespoon chopped
fresh **coriander leaves**

This juice is ideal for fighting the common effects of colds and flu. This is a powerful spicy juice, so be prepared!

1 Scrub the carrots. Deseed the chilli. Cut off the skin and tough core of the pineapple and cut the flesh into chunks. Juice the carrots, chilli or chilli powder and pineapple.

2 Pour the juice into a tall glass over ice, stir in the lime juice and chopped coriander leaves and serve immediately.

240 Kcals

vit C

revive

152 juices

Celery, tomato and lemon

This vibrant, fresh-tasting juice is packed full of nutrients. It will provide 15 per cent of your daily requirement of calcium and is also an excellent source of iron.

1 Cut the celery into 5 cm (2 inch) lengths. Juice the tomatoes, parsley and lemon rind and juice with the celery.

2 Pour the juice into a tall glass over ice and serve immediately.

Makes 300 ml (½ pint)

2 **celery sticks**

4 **tomatoes**

large handful of **parsley**

rind and juice of ½ **lemon**

ice cubes

82 Kcals

iron

boost

Ginger
and garlic

Makes 150 ml (¼ pint)

175 g (6 oz) **carrots**

2.5 cm (1 inch) cube
fresh root ginger

100 g (3½ oz) **celery**, plus
extra to serve (optional)

300 g (10 oz) **tomatoes**

1 **garlic clove**

2.5 cm (1 inch) cube
fresh **horseradish**

ice cubes

This spicy juice makes a real change from some of the sweeter drinks. Tomatoes and carrots provide large amounts of vitamin C, essential for maintaining a healthy body. Garlic, ginger and horseradish are all powerful antioxidants.

1 Scrub the carrots. Peel and roughly chop the ginger. Trim the celery and cut it into 5 cm (2 inch) lengths. Juice the tomatoes, garlic and horseradish with the carrots, ginger and celery.

2 Transfer the juice to a blender, add a couple of ice cubes and process briefly.

3 Pour the juice into a tall glass and serve immediately, garnished with slivers of celery, if liked.

189 Kcals

vit A

energize

Celery, tomato and red pepper

This zingy vegetable juice will provide you with a real boost and is a fabulously colourful drink to serve to friends.

1 Trim the celery and cut it into 5 cm (2 inch) lengths. Chop the tomatoes and red pepper into chunks and juice them with the celery.

2 Deseed and finely chop the chilli and crush the garlic (if used) and mix them into the juice.

3 Pour the juice into a glass, add a couple of ice cubes, if liked, and serve immediately.

Makes 300 ml (½ pint)

4 **celery sticks**

3 ripe **tomatoes**

½ **red pepper**

½ **red chilli**, deseeded (optional)

1 **garlic clove**, crushed (optional)

ice cubes (optional)

83 Kcals

vit C

boost

Carrot and sweet potato

Makes 200 ml (7 fl oz)

175 g (6 oz) **carrots**

175 g (6 oz) **parsnips**

175 g (6 oz) **celery**

175 g (6 oz) **sweet potato**

handful **parsley**, plus extra to serve (optional)

1 **garlic clove**

ice cubes

lemon wedges, to serve (optional)

This is a brilliant all-rounder of a juice that also tasted deliciously sweet.

1 Scrub the carrots and parsnips. Trim the celery and cut it into 5 cm (2 inch) lengths. Chop the sweet potato into chunks. Juice the vegetables with the parsley and garlic.

2 Transfer the juice to a blender, add a couple of ice cubes and process briefly.

3 Pour the juice into a tall glass and serve immediately, garnished with a wedge of lemon and a sprig of parsley, if liked.

386 Kcals

vit A

calm

156 juices

Carrot, orange and apple

A delicious combination of flavours, this juice is a good source of vitamins and fibre. Choose a tart apple, such as Granny Smith, to counterbalance the sweetness of the carrot juice.

1 Scrub the carrots. Peel the orange and divide into segments. Cut the carrots and apple into evenly sized pieces. Juice all the fruit.

2 Pour the juice into a tall glass over ice and serve immediately.

Makes 250 ml (8 fl oz)

200 g (7 oz) **carrots**
1 **orange**
1 **apple**
ice cubes

160 Kcals

vit C

boost

Beetroot, celery and apple

Makes 150 ml (¼ pint)

50 g (2 oz) **beetroot**

75 g (3 oz) **celery**

200 g (7 oz) **apple**, plus extra to serve (optional)

ice cubes

This is a super cleansing juice for the whole system, perfect if you have been overindulging!

1 Scrub the beetroot. Cut the celery into 5 cm (2 inch) lengths. Cut the apples into chunks and juice them with the beetroot and celery.

2 Pour the juice into a tall glass over ice and serve immediately, decorated with slices of apple, if liked.

179 Kcals

folic acid

cleanse

Celery, apple and alfalfa

This juice contains folic acid and is therefore particularly beneficial to women. Although it provides good amounts of vitamins A, C and K, alfalfa is rather bitter on its own and needs to be combined, as here, with sweeter flavours.

1 Cut the celery into 5 cm (2 inch) lengths. Chop the apple into chunks. Rinse the alfalfa. Juice the celery with the apple and alfalfa, alternating the ingredients to make sure that the machine doesn't get clogged up.

2 Pour the juice into a tall glass over ice and serve immediately.

Makes 250 ml (8 fl oz)

3 **celery sticks**
2 **apples**
25 g (1 oz) **alfalfa**
ice cubes

106 Kcals

vit A

energize

Asparagus and dandelion

Makes 200 ml (7 fl oz)

125 g (4 oz) **asparagus** spears

10 **dandelion leaves**

175 g (6 oz) **cucumber**

200 g (7 oz) **pear**

125 g (4 oz) **melon**

ice cubes

All the ingredients in this juice contain high levels of zinc and potassium. The juice is therefore beneficial for liver and kidney function and may help alleviate bloating.

1 Trim the woody bits off the asparagus spears. Roll the dandelion leaves into a ball and juice them (if you have picked wild leaves, wash them thoroughly first) with the asparagus. Juice the cucumber and pear with their skins.

2 Remove the skin and seeds from the melon and chop the flesh into chunks. Transfer the juice to a blender, add the melon and process briefly.

3 Pour the juice into a tall glass over ice and serve immediately.

160 juices

215 Kcals

zinc

soothe

Beetroot, apple and carrot

Vitamin C, folic acid and iron are all essential nutrients, making this juice a good choice for anyone who exercises.

1 Scrub the beetroot and carrots and cut them into chunks. Chop the apple into pieces and juice with the beetroot and carrots.

2 Mix the juice with the water, pour it into a tall glass over ice and serve immediately.

Makes 300 ml (½ pint)

1 small **beetroot**

50 g (2 oz) **carrots**

1 **apple**

150 ml (¼ pint) **water**

ice cubes

83
Kcals

folic acid

energize

Beetroot
and fennel

Makes 200 ml (7 fl oz)

175 g (6 oz) **carrots**

100 g (3½ oz) **beetroot**

175 g (6 oz) **yams** or
sweet potatoes

125 g (4 oz) **fennel**, plus
fronds to serve (optional)

ice cubes

The strong flavour of the fennel in this juice cuts through the earthiness of the other vegetables. As an added benefit to the great taste, this juice may be particularly beneficial for hormone imbalances.

1 Scrub the carrots and beetroot. Chop the yams or sweet potatoes into chunks and juice them with the carrots, beetroot and fennel.

2 Pour the juice into a tall glass over ice and serve immediately, garnished with fennel fronds, if liked.

296 Kcals

iron

boost

Carrot and kiwifruit

The sharpness of the kiwifruit helps to cut through the sweetness of the carrot juice in this refreshing drink.

1 Scrub the carrots. Cut the carrots and kiwifruit (there is no need to peel it) into evenly sized pieces and juice them.

2 Pour the juice into a tall glass over ice and serve immediately, decorated with slices of kiwifruit, if liked.

Makes 250 ml (8 fl oz)

200 g (7 oz) **carrots**

1 **kiwifruit**, plus extra to serve (optional)

ice cubes

99
Kcals

vit C

energize

Pineapple and blackberry

Makes 200 ml (7 fl oz)

375 g (12 oz) **pineapple**, plus extra to serve (optional)

375 g (12 oz) **blackberries**

ice cubes

Pineapples can aid digestion and help reduce inflammation in body tissue. Good results from a delicious drink.

1 Remove the skin and tough core of the pineapple and cut the flesh into chunks. Juice the blackberries, then the pineapple.

2 Transfer the juice to a blender, add a couple of ice cubes and process briefly.

3 Pour the juice into a tall glass and serve immediately, decorated with a sliver of pineapple, if liked.

353 Kcals

folic acid

refresh

Avocado
and apricot

This juice contains avocados which are packed with the antioxidant vitamins A, C and E. Dried apricots are an excellent source of beta-carotene, iron, potassium, calcium and magnesium.

1 Remove the skin and seeds from the melon and juice the flesh with the cucumber.

2 Remove the peel and stone from the avocado and put the flesh in a blender. Add the juice, apricots, wheatgerm and a couple of ice cubes and process it all briefly.

3 Pour the juice into a tall glass and serve immediately, decorated with slivers of dried apricot, if liked.

Makes 200 ml (7 fl oz)

175 g (6 oz) **melon**

125 g (4 oz) **cucumber**

125 g (4 oz) **avocado**

50 g (2 oz) ready-to-eat **dried apricots**, plus extra to serve (optional)

1 tablespoon **wheatgerm**

ice cubes

357 Kcals

vit E

revive

Watercress and pear

Makes 250 ml (8 fl oz)

40 g (1½ oz) **watercress**

3 ripe **pears**

ice cubes

This juice is rich in several important nutrients. It is ideal for topping up fluids before and during many sports. It's also fantastically easy to make, so you can prepare it quickly before you rush out the door.

1 Wash the watercress and drain it thoroughly. Wash the pears and cut them into evenly sized pieces. Juice the pears and watercress, alternating them to make sure that the machine doesn't get clogged up.

2 Pour the juice into a tall glass over ice and serve immediately.

70 Kcals

vit C

boost

Melon and cucumber

This a delightfully light and refreshing juice that is perfect for cleansing the system.

1 Remove the skin from the melon, but leave the seeds, and chop the flesh into chunks. Juice the cucumber and cranberries with the melon.

2 Pour the juice into a tall glass and serve decorated with melon sticks, if liked.

Makes 200 ml (7 fl oz)

250 g (8 oz) **watermelon** or **galia melon**, plus extra to serve (optional)

250 g (8 oz) **cucumber**

250 g (8 oz) **cranberries**

232 Kcals

calcium

cleanse

Carrot and apricot

Makes 200 ml (7 fl oz)

150 g (5 oz) **carrots**

100 g (3½ oz) **orange**

100 g (3½ oz) **banana**

6 ready-to-eat **dried apricots**

ice cubes

Full of iron, calcium and potassium, this non-dairy juice is great for bones and teeth, and for keeping colds at bay. Bananas have calming properties, so this is a good drink for the end of a busy day.

1 Scrub the carrots and juice them together with the orange.

2 Transfer the juice to a blender, add the banana, apricots and a couple of ice cubes and process it all briefly.

3 Pour the juice into a tall glass and serve immediately.

204 Kcals

calcium

revive

Beetroot
and berry

This deep red juice is a real booster for your blood. Beetroot builds up red blood cells and the berries contain natural aspirin, which can help protect against clots and strokes.

1 Scrub the beetroot and juice it.

2 Transfer the beetroot juice to a blender, add the blueberries, raspberries and a couple of ice cubes and process until smooth.

3 Pour the juice into a tall glass and serve immediately, decorated with blueberries, if liked.

Makes 250 ml (8 fl oz)

50 g (2 oz) **beetroot**

100 g (3½ oz) **blueberries**, plus extra to serve (optional)

100 g (3½ oz) **raspberries**

ice cubes

75 Kcals

calcium

energize

juices **169**

Avocado and pear

Makes 200 ml (7 fl oz)

375 g (12 oz) **pears**

75 g (3 oz) **avocado**

ice cubes

Using avocado in a juice creates a smoother texture which is much more luxurious than some of the thinner juices.

1 Wash the pears, chop them into chunks and juice them.

2 Peel the avocado, remove the stone and chop the flesh. Transfer the pear juice to a blender, add the avocado and a couple of ice cubes and process it all until smooth.

3 Pour the juice into a tall glass and serve immediately.

290 Kcals

folate

soothe

Strawberry and spirulina

High in potassium, vitamins C and B12, and essential fatty acids, this juice packs a punch. Banana helps to rebalance your sugar levels and provide energy. Protein in the linseeds also regulates sugar levels. The amount of vitamin B in this juice will also increase your energy levels.

1 Hull the strawberries and juice them with the kiwifruit (there is no need to peel it).

2 Transfer the juice to a blender, add the banana, spirulina, linseeds and a couple of ice cubes and process until smooth.

3 Pour the drink into a tall glass and serve immediately, decorated with redcurrants, if liked.

Makes 200 ml (7 fl oz)

250 g (8 oz) **strawberries**

125 g (4 oz) **kiwifruit**

100 g (3½ oz) **banana**

1 tablespoon **spirulina**

1 tablespoon **linseeds**

ice cubes

redcurrants, to decorate (optional)

252 Kcals

vit C

energize

Mango, apple and cucumber

Makes 200 ml (7 fl oz)

100 g (3½ oz) **mango**
200 g (7 oz) **apple**
125 g (4 oz) **cucumber**
ice cubes

Cucumber is extremely hydrating; combining it with sweet mango and apple creates a delicious cooling drink that is perfect for summer days.

1 Peel the mango and remove the stone. Peel the apple and cucumber. Juice the mango with the apple and cucumber.

2 Transfer the juice to a blender, add a couple of ice cubes and process briefly.

3 Pour the juice into a tall glass and serve immediately.

vit A

refresh

200
Kcals

Pineapple
and orange

This really flavoursome juice is absolutely packed with complex carbohydrates, which play an important role in maintaining a healthy balanced diet.

1 Remove the skin and tough core from the pineapple and chop the flesh into chunks. Juice the grapes, orange and apple with the pineapple.

2 Peel the mango, remove the stone and roughly chop the flesh. Peel the banana.

3 Transfer the juice to a blender, add the mango, banana and a couple of ice cubes and process until smooth.

4 Pour the juice into a tall glass and serve immediately, decorated with orange wedges and a sprig of mint.

Makes 400 ml (14 fl oz)

100 g (3½ oz) **pineapple**

100 g (3½ oz) seedless **green grapes**

100 g (3½ oz) **orange**, plus extra to serve

100 g (3½ oz) **apple**

100 g (3½ oz) **mango**

100 g (3½ oz) **banana**

ice cubes

sprig of **mint**, to serve

383
Kcals

vit A

satisfy

Carrot, ginger and beetroot

Makes 1.3 litres
(2¼ pints)

10 large **carrots**

4 large **beetroots**

2.5 cm (1 inch) piece of
fresh root ginger

You will need a good fruit and vegetable juicer for this recipe, so that all the nutrients from the ingredients are extracted into a smooth and silky drink. You can vary this juice by using 4–6 apples instead of the beetroots.

1 Scrub the carrots and beetroots and peel the ginger. Put them all through a juicer.

2 Strain, if liked, into a tall glass and serve immediately.

785
Kcals

folic acid

energize

174 juices

Pineapple and grape

Both pineapples and grapes give a boost of blood sugar, which can help to induce sleep. Lettuce and celery relax the nerves and muscles, making this an ideal juice if you are having difficulty getting to sleep.

1 Remove the skin and tough core from the pineapple. Separate the lettuce leaves. Trim the celery and cut it into 5 cm (2 inch) lengths. Juice the grapes with the pineapple, lettuce and celery.

2 Pour into a tall glass over ice and serve immediately, decorated with lettuce leaves, if liked.

Makes 200 ml (7 fl oz)

125 g (4 oz) **pineapple**

50 g (2 oz) **lettuce**, plus extra to serve (optional)

50 g (2 oz) **celery**

125 g (4 oz) **green grapes**

ice cubes

167 Kcals

vit C

soothe

Apple and pear

Makes 200 ml (7 fl oz)

2 **pears**

2 **apples**

ice cubes

As well as being a vitamin-enriched tonic, this juice is an excellent natural laxative. For added potency, stir in a couple of tablespoons of prune juice and nibble a handful of pumpkin seeds.

1 Roughly chop the pears and apples, including the cores, and juice them.

2 Transfer the juice to a blender, add a couple of ice cubes and process until smooth.

3 Pour into a tall glass and serve.

180 Kcals

copper

boost

176 juices

Orange
and celery

The beta-carotene in carrots is believed to promote good eyesight, especially night vision. Orange adds an extra sweetness to the juice.

1 Trim the celery and cut it into 5 cm (2 inch) lengths. Scrub the carrots. Juice the tomatoes and oranges with the celery and carrots.

2 Pour the juice into 2 glasses over ice and serve immediately with leafy celery stalk stirrers.

Makes 400 ml (14 fl oz)

2 **celery sticks**, plus leafy stalks, to serve

2 **carrots**

4 **tomatoes**

2 **oranges**

ice cubes

63 Kcals

folate

energize

Broccoli and apple

Makes 300 ml (½ pint)

200 g 7 oz) **broccoli**

200 g (7 oz) **apple**, such as Braeburn or Cox

50 g (2 oz) **spinach**

50 g (2 oz) **green grapes**

ice cubes

This juice is full of iron, vitamin **K** and magnesium, which help to maintain strong bones and teeth.

1 Roughly chop the broccoli and quarter the apples. Juice them with the spinach and grapes.

2 Transfer the juice to a blender and process briefly with a couple of ice cubes.

3 Pour into 2 glasses and serve immediately.

100 Kcals

iron

boost

Strawberry and pineapple

This fruity drink delivers a potent shot of potassium and vitamin C into your body, and will help boost your immune system. The banana makes it taste really creamy and indulgent.

1 Hull the strawberries. Peel the pineapple, remove the central core and roughly chop the flesh. Juice the strawberries with the pineapple.

2 Peel and chop the banana. Transfer the juice into a blender, add the banana and a couple of ice cubes and process until smooth.

3 Pour the juice into a tall glass and serve immediately, decorated with strawberries.

Makes 300 ml (½ pint)

100 g (3½ oz) **strawberries**, plus extra to serve

300 g (10 oz) **pineapple**

1 **banana**

ice cubes

190 Kcals

vit C

revive

smoothies

Banana
and mango

Makes 600 ml (1 pint)

1 large **banana**, plus
extra to serve (optional)

1 large ripe **mango**

150 ml (¼ pint)
natural yogurt

300 ml (½ pint)
pineapple juice

Both bananas and mangoes supply fibre, making
this a filling and satisfying smoothie. The yogurt
provides calcium, which is essential for bone health
and strength.

1 Peel and slice the banana and freeze the pieces
for at least 2 hours or overnight.

2 Peel the mango, remove the stone and cube the
flesh. Put the frozen banana, mango, yogurt and
pineapple juice into a blender and process until
smooth and creamy.

3 Pour the smoothie into 2 glasses and serve
immediately, decorated with slices of banana,
if liked.

230
Kcals

fibre

satisfy

Banana and chocolate

This should satisfy any cravings for an additive-ridden, sugary milkshake. It's a bit naughty, but far healthier than the versions you find in burger-bars.

1 Peel and roughly chop the banana. Put all the ingredients in a blender and process until smooth and creamy.

2 Pour the smoothie into 2 tall glasses and serve immediately, dusted with cocoa powder, if liked.

Makes 650 ml (22 fl oz)

1 **banana**

2 tablespoons **cocoa powder**, plus extra to serve (optional)

300 ml (½ pint) **semi-skimmed milk**

100 ml (3½ fl oz) **apple juice**

2 large scoops **vanilla ice cream**

600 Kcals

calcium

energize

Kiwifruit and strawberry

Makes 300 ml (½ pint)

100 g (3½ oz) fresh or frozen **strawberries**

200 ml (7 fl oz) **soya milk**

2 **kiwifruit**

25 g (1 oz) **flaked almonds**, plus extra to serve (optional)

ice cubes (optional)

If you can't sleep, this delicious smoothie at bedtime should be beneficial. Soya milk and almonds both help to alleviate insomnia, calm nerves and help to combat depression.

1 Hull the strawberries. Put the milk and kiwifruit (there is no need to peel them) together with the strawberries and almonds in a blender. If you are using fresh rather than frozen strawberries, add a few ice cubes, then process until smooth.

2 Pour the smoothie into a tall glass and serve immediately, decorated with flaked almonds, if liked.

300 Kcals

vit C

soothe

Peaches
and cream

This winning combination is a great way to add more calcium to your diet. It can easily be adapted to a store-cupboard version using canned peaches or apricots, or you can substitute nectarines for the peaches if they are more readily available.

1 Peel the peach, remove the stone and roughly chop the flesh.

2 Put the peach, yogurt and milk into a blender and process until smooth.

3 Pour the smoothie into a tall glass and serve decorated with raspberries.

Makes 200 ml (7 fl oz)

1 large **peach**

150 ml (¼ pint) **natural yogurt**

50 ml (2 fl oz) **milk**

a few **raspberries**, to serve

150 Kcals

calcium

boost

Banana and avocado

Makes 300 ml (½ pint)

1 small ripe **avocado**

1 small ripe **banana**

250 ml (8 fl oz) **skimmed milk**

ice cubes

pieces of **pineapple**, to serve (optional)

This creamy smoothie is almost a meal in itself. It's an excellent choice if you are recuperating from illness because avocados are considered a complete food that is easy to digest. Combined with banana and milk, they are great for repair.

1 Peel the avocado and remove the stone. Peel and slice the banana.

2 Put the avocado, banana and milk in a blender and process until smooth.

3 Pour the smoothie into a tall glass, add a couple of ice cubes and serve immediately, decorated with a piece of pineapple, if liked.

270 Kcals

vit K

energize

Papaya
and banana

This is a refreshing pick-me-up. Use a 400 g (13 oz) can of apricot halves in natural juice instead of the papaya and apple juice for a convenient store-cupboard version.

1 Halve and deseed the papaya, scoop out the flesh with a spoon and put it in a blender.

2 Peel and slice the banana, and peel and segment the orange. Add the banana and orange to the blender with the apple juice and a couple of ice cubes and process until smooth.

3 Pour the smoothie into 2 tall glasses and serve immediately.

Makes 400 ml (14 fl oz)

1 **papaya**

1 **banana**

1 **orange**

300 ml (½ pint) **apple juice**

ice cubes

190 Kcals

vit C

refresh

Passion fruit and watermelon

Makes 150 ml (¼ pint)

about 150 g (5 oz) **watermelon**

1 **kiwifruit**

100 ml (3½ fl oz) **passion fruit juice**

This is a deliciously sweet yet refreshing drink and great for rehydration when energy levels are all used up. If you cannot find passion fruit juice, try using pineapple juice instead.

1 Remove the skin and, if you want, the seeds from the watermelon, chop the flesh into chunks and freeze it for at least 2 hours or overnight.

2 Peel and roughly chop the kiwifruit, put the pieces in a blender with the watermelon and passion fruit juice and process it all until thick and smooth.

3 Pour the juice into a tall glass and serve immediately.

125 Kcals

vit A

revive

Peach and orange

This healthy smoothie is so quick and simple to make that it can be ready in a minute. It's high in calcium and immune-boosting beta-carotene.

1 Put the peaches in a blender with the yogurt, orange juice and honey (if used) and process it all until smooth.

2 Pour the smoothie into a tall glass over ice, top with a swirl of any remaining yogurt and serve immediately.

Makes 200 ml (7 fl oz)

200 g (7 oz) can **peaches** in natural juice, drained

75 ml (3 fl oz) peach or apricot **yogurt**, plus extra to serve

100 ml (3½ fl oz) **orange juice**

1 teaspoon **clear honey** (optional)

ice cubes

170 Kcals

calcium

boost

Banana
and almond

Makes 300 ml (½ pint)

1 ripe **banana**

250 ml (8 fl oz) **soya milk**

20 g (¾ oz) **ground almonds**

pinch of **ground cinnamon**, plus extra to serve

1 teaspoon **clear honey** (optional)

ice cubes

The combination of bananas, ground almonds and soya milk makes this a highly nutritious drink. It is best to use ripe bananas because less ripe ones are less digestible.

1 Peel and slice the banana and freeze it for at least 2 hours or overnight.

2 Put the frozen banana, milk, ground almonds and cinnamon in a blender, add the honey (if used) and process until thick and frothy.

3 Pour the smoothie into a glass, add a couple of ice cubes and serve immediately with a dusting of cinnamon.

315 Kcals

vit E

energize

Blackcurrant and soya

This creamy smoothie is bursting with vitamin C, which makes it a great choice when you feel like a low-carb treat. Blackcurrants are one of the best sources of vitamin C, providing four times the quantity found in the equivalent weight of oranges.

1 Remove the stalks and tops from the blackcurrants. Put the fruit in a blender with the cream cheese and milk. Add the ice cubes and a squeeze of lemon juice and process until smooth.

2 Pour the smoothie into a tall glass and serve immediately, decorated with blackcurrants.

Makes 200 ml (7 fl oz)

75 g (3 oz) **blackcurrants**, plus extra to serve

50 g (2 oz) **cream cheese**

100 ml (3½ fl oz) **soya milk**

2 **ice cubes**

squeeze of **lemon juice**

272 Kcals

vit C

soothe

Cherry and chocolate

Makes 250 ml (8 fl oz)

100 g (3½ oz) **cherries**

100 ml (3½ fl oz) **soya milk**

30 g (1¼ oz) chocolate-flavoured **whey protein powder**

2–3 **ice cubes**

cocoa powder, to serve

This is a rather indulgent smoothie, but you can salve your conscience by remember that cherries are a top source of antioxidants.

1 Pit the cherries and put them in a blender. Pour in the milk, add the whey protein powder and the ice cubes and process until smooth.

2 Pour the smoothie into a glass and serve immediately with a dusting of cocoa powder.

173 Kcals

calcium

satisfy

Cucumber and mint

This light but refreshing smoothie is great for health as it stimulates the elimination of toxins.

1 Peel and roughly dice the cucumber and mix it with the lemon juice.

2 Transfer the cucumber and lemon to a blender, add the mint leaves and a couple of ice cubes and process until smooth.

3 Pour the smoothie into a tall glass and serve immediately, garnished with mint leaves, if liked.

Makes 300 ml (½ pint)

250 g (8 oz) **cucumber**

2 tablespoons **lemon juice**

3–4 fresh **mint leaves**, plus extra to serve (optional)

ice cubes

27 Kcals

calcium

refresh

Blackberry and grape

Makes 200 ml (7 fl oz)

125 g (4 oz) frozen **blackberries**

300 ml (½ pint) purple **grape juice**

3 tablespoons **quark** or **fromage frais**

1 teaspoon **clear honey** (optional)

Blackberries and purple grape juice contain antioxidants that are important for general health. Adding quark or fromage frais gives this drink a creamy taste and texture and also boosts its calcium and protein content.

1 Put the blackberries, grape juice and quark or fromage frais in a blender, add the honey (if used) and process until smooth and thick.

2 Pour the smoothie into a tall glass and serve immediately.

200 Kcals

vit C

satisfy

Mango, banana and orange

Bananas are a perfect base for a creamy smoothie and brilliant for really active people because they are rich in carbohydrate and potassium.

1 Peel and slice the banana. Peel the mango, remove the stone and roughly chop the flesh.

2 Put the banana, mango, orange juice, milk, fromage frais and a couple of ice cubes in a blender and process until smooth.

3 Pour the smoothie into 2 tall glasses and serve immediately.

Makes 400 ml (14 fl oz)

1 ripe **banana**

1 ripe **mango**

200 ml (7 fl oz) **orange juice**

200 ml (7 fl oz) **semi-skimmed milk**

3 tablespoons **fromage frais**

ice cubes

190 Kcals

vit A

energize

Mango
and melon

Makes 400 ml (14 fl oz)

1 ripe **mango**

about 300 g (10 oz)
galia melon

200 ml (7 fl oz)
orange juice

ice cubes

Packed with iron, calcium and potassium, this all-round booster is great for bones and teeth. It is also really energizing when combined with a protein snack, such as nuts and seeds.

1 Peel the mango, remove the stone and roughly chop the flesh. Remove the skin and seeds from the melon and chop the flesh into chunks.

2 Put the mango and melon flesh in a blender, add the orange juice and a couple of ice cubes and process until smooth.

3 Pour the juice into 2 tall glasses and serve immediately.

115 Kcals

iron

energize

Apricot
and cream

This smoothie is an excellent source of calcium, providing almost one-third of the daily requirement. Canned apricots in natural juice are a useful store-cupboard standby and provide an extra source of carbohydrate.

1 Drain the apricots, put them in a blender with the yogurt and milk and process until smooth.

2 Pour the smoothie into 2 tall glasses and serve immediately, decorated with slices of apricot, if liked.

Makes 300 ml (½ pint)

200 g (7 oz) can **apricots** in natural juice, plus extra to serve (optional)

150 ml (¼ pint) **apricot yogurt**

150 ml (¼ pint) ice-cold **semi-skimmed milk**

140 Kcals

calcium

boost

Blackcurrant and honey

Makes 400 ml (14 fl oz)

200 g (7 oz)
blackcurrants

100 ml (3½ fl oz)
apple juice

300 ml (½ pint)
natural yogurt

2 tablespoons
clear honey

If you are lactose intolerant or suffer regularly with colds and sinus problems, use soya yogurt as a replacement. You can also use strawberries or blackberries instead of the blackcurrants.

1 Remove any stalks from the blackcurrants and reserve a few. Freeze the remainder for at least 2 hours or overnight.

2 Put the frozen blackcurrants in a blender with the apple juice and half the yogurt and process until smooth.

3 Pour the smoothie into 2 tall glasses. Combine the rest of the yogurt with the honey, spoon the mixture over the smoothie and serve immediately, decorated with the reserved fruit.

200 Kcals

calcium

revive

Kiwifruit and mango

This colourful smoothie is an excellent source of many nutrients and you can vary the fruit you use to get a different layered effect.

1 Peel and roughly chop the kiwifruit. Put the flesh in a blender and process it until it is smooth, then spoon it into 2 tall glasses. Top each with a spoonful of yogurt, spreading the yogurt to the sides of the glasses.

2 Peel the mango, remove the stone and roughly chop the flesh. Put it in a blender with the orange or apple juice and process until smooth. Spoon it into the glasses and top with a layer of yogurt.

3 Put the raspberries in the blender and process briefly, then push the purée through a sieve to extract the seeds. Check the sweetness of the purée and add a little honey if necessary. Spoon the raspberry purée into the glasses and serve immediately.

Makes 400 ml (14 fl oz)

3 **kiwifruit**

150 ml (¼ pint) **lemon or orange yogurt**

1 small **mango**

2 tablespoons **orange juice** or **apple juice**

150 g (5 oz) **raspberries**

1–2 teaspoons **clear honey** (optional)

170 Kcals

vit C

energize

Summer berry

Makes 300 ml (½ pint)

150 g (5 oz) frozen mixed **summer berries**, plus extra to serve (optional)

300 ml (½ pint) vanilla-flavoured **soya milk**

1 teaspoon **clear honey** (optional)

Summer berries are packed with vitamins C and B. Their deep colour and rich flavour make them ideal for including in smoothies. Nutritionally, frozen fruit is every bit as good as fresh, and it is available all year round.

1 Put the berries, milk and honey (if used) in a blender and process until thick.

2 Pour the smoothie into 2 glasses and serve immediately, decorated with extra berries, if liked.

160 Kcals

vit C

revive

Banana and sunflower

When you want a quick meal, you will find this easy-to-prepare drink high in a number of nutrients.

1 Peel the banana and put it in a blender. Add the orange juice, sunflower seeds and a couple of ice cubes and process until smooth.

2 Pour the juice into a tall glass and serve decorated with some strawberry halves, if liked.

Makes 300 ml (½ pint)

1 small **banana**

200 ml (7 fl oz) **orange juice**

25 g (1 oz) **sunflower seeds**

ice cubes

strawberries, to serve (optional)

340 Kcals

vit E

soothe

Avocado
and chilli

Makes 200 ml (7 fl oz)

30 g (1¼ oz) **spring onions**

½ small **chilli**

½ **avocado**

100 ml (3½ fl oz) **tomato juice**

handful of fresh **coriander leaves**, plus extra to serve

ice cubes

This Mexican-inspired savoury drink is full of nutrients and low in carbs. The combination of tomato and avocado provides a good boost of antioxidants.

1 Trim and roughly chop the spring onions. Deseed and chop the chilli. Peel the avocado, remove the stone and chop the flesh into chunks. Put the spring onions, chilli and avocado in a blender, add the tomato juice, coriander leaves and a couple of ice cubes and process until smooth.

2 Pour the juice into a tall glass and serve immediately, garnished with chopped coriander.

167 Kcals

calcium

revive

Blueberry and raspberry

Take some time to present this smoothie carefully: it's worth the effort. It's tasty, bursting with nutrients and makes a wonderful breakfast treat.

1 Put the raspberries in a blender with half the apple juice and process to make a smooth purée. Transfer the purée to a bowl. Purée the blueberries with the remaining apple juice and transfer to another bowl.

2 Mix together the yogurt, milk, honey and wheatgerm (if used) and add a spoonful of the raspberry purée.

3 Pour the blueberry purée into a tall glass. Carefully pour over the yogurt mixture and then pour the raspberry purée over the surface of the yogurt. Chill before serving.

Makes 900 ml (1½ pints)

250 g (8 oz) **raspberries**

200 ml (7 fl oz) **apple juice**

200 g (7 oz) **blueberries**

4 tablespoons **Greek yogurt**

100 ml (3½ fl oz) **skimmed milk**

1 tablespoon **clear honey**, or to taste

1 tablespoon **wheatgerm** (optional)

510 Kcals

iron

satisfy

Apricot
and almond

Makes 200 ml (7 fl oz)

100 g (3½ oz) **apricots**

30 g (1¼ oz)
ground almonds

50 ml (2 fl oz) **soya milk**

50 g (2 oz) **soya yogurt**

ice cubes

chopped almonds,
to serve

This smoothie is highly nutritious: apricots are full
of beta-carotene, and almonds are a concentrated
source of protein, unsaturated fats and minerals.

1 Skin the apricots, remove the stones and roughly
chop the flesh. Put it in a blender with the ground
almonds, milk, yogurt and a couple of ice cubes and
process until smooth and creamy.

2 Pour the smoothie into a tall glass and serve
immediately, decorated with chopped almonds.

250
Kcals

vit A

energize

Cranberry and yogurt

This delicious smoothie is excellent for the kidneys and high in bone-boosting calcium. Cranberries may also help promote good heart health, inhibit cancerous cell growth and counteract the effects of premature ageing.

1 Put the cranberries in a blender, add the yogurt, milk and a couple of ice cubes and process until smooth. Taste, then add artificial sweetener if required and process again.

2 Pour the smoothie into a tall glass and serve immediately.

Makes 300 ml (½ pint)

100 g (3½ oz) **cranberries**

50 g (2 oz) **Greek yogurt**

100 ml (3½ fl oz) **soya milk**

ice cubes

artificial **sweetener** (optional)

100 Kcals

calcium

boost

Melon and almond

Makes 250 ml (8 fl oz)

100 g (3½ oz)
galia melon, plus
extra to serve

100 ml (3½ fl oz) **almond milk**

This calming and refreshing smoothie is perfect at the end of a hard day or after strenuous exercise. Almonds are rich in the monounsaturated fats that help protect against heart disease by lowering blood cholesterol levels.

1 Remove the skin and seeds from the melon, chop the flesh into chunks and freeze it for at least 2 hours or overnight.

2 Put the frozen melon in a blender with the milk and process until smooth and creamy.

3 Pour the smoothie into a tall glass and serve immediately, decorated with a melon slice.

24 Kcals

vit C

soothe

Dried fruit

This excellent smoothie is great for refuelling and increase energy levels when you are feeling drained and hungry.

1 Roughly chop the dried fruit salad and put it in a large bowl. Pour over the apple juice, cover the bowl and allow to stand overnight.

2 Put the fruit and apple juice in a blender, add the yogurt and process until smooth, adding a little more apple juice if necessary.

3 Pour the smoothie into a tall glass, add a couple of ice cubes, if liked, and serve immediately.

Makes 250 ml (8 fl oz)

25 g (2 oz) **dried fruit salad**

about 200 ml (7 fl oz) **apple juice**

100 ml (3½ fl oz) **Greek yogurt**

ice cubes (optional)

140 Kcals

calcium

boost

Rhubarb
and yogurt

Makes 200 ml (7 fl oz)

100 g (3½ oz) stewed **rhubarb**

100 g (3½ oz) **natural yogurt**

2 drops of **vanilla extract**

artificial **sweetener**, to taste

ice cubes

Rhubarb must be cooked because it is full of oxalic acid when raw. Combined with yogurt, it makes a delicious smoothie that is full of friendly bacteria.

1 Put the stewed rhubarb in a blender, add the yogurt, vanilla extract, artificial sweetener and a couple of ice cubes and process until smooth.

2 Pour the smoothie into a tall glass and serve immediately.

48 Kcals

calcium

revive

Strawberry and pineapple

Like many smoothies, this one is a great way of restoring energy. It contains a high level of calcium, which is essential for healthy bones and helps to maintain normal blood pressure.

1 Hull and roughly chop the strawberries and freeze them for at least 2 hours or overnight.

2 Put the frozen strawberries, pineapple juice and yogurt in a blender and process until smooth.

3 Pour the smoothie into a tall glass over ice and serve immediately, decorated with strawberries, if liked.

Makes 400 ml (14 fl oz)

150 g (5 oz) **strawberries**, plus extra to serve (optional)

150 ml (¼ pint) **pineapple juice**

150 g (5 oz) **strawberry yogurt**

ice cubes

260 Kcals

calcium

boost

Peach and tofu

Makes 150 ml (¼ pint)

50 g (2 oz) **peach**

50 g (2 oz) **tofu**

25 g (1 oz) **vanilla ice cream**

50 ml (2 fl oz) **water**

few drops of **almond essence**

ice cubes (optional)

This smoothie has the taste of summer and is made extra creamy by the addition of homemade ice cream.

1 Remove the skin and stone from the peach and roughly chop the flesh. Put it in a blender with the tofu and the ice cream, add the water and almond essence and process until smooth.

2 Pour the smoothie into a glasses over ice, if liked, and serve immediately.

 230 Kcals

 calcium

 energize

Strawberry and peanut butter

If you want a quick breakfast replacement, this is the perfect smoothie. It is full of protein and will easily keep you going until lunchtime.

1 Hull and roughly chop the strawberries and put them in a blender. Spoon in the peanut butter and whey protein powder, add the water and a couple of ice cubes and process until smooth and creamy.

2 Pour the smoothie into a glass and serve immediately, decorated with half a strawberry, if liked.

Makes 300 ml (½ pint)

100 g (3½ oz) **strawberries**, plus extra to serve (optional)

25 g (1 oz) smooth **peanut butter**

25 g (1 oz) **whey protein powder**

150 ml (¼ pint) **water**

ice cubes

282 Kcals

vit C

satisfy

Coconut and pineapple

Makes 300 ml (½ pint)

100 g (3½ oz) **pineapple**

100 ml (3½ fl oz) **coconut milk**

100 ml (3½ fl oz) **soya milk**

½ teaspoon **toasted coconut**, to serve

If you like pina coladas, you'll love this tasty smoothie. You could also add a few drops of rum flavouring for extra authenticity.

1 Peel the pineapple and remove the tough core. Chop the flesh into chunks and freeze for at least 2 hours or overnight.

2 Put the frozen pineapple in a blender, add the coconut and soya milks and process until smooth.

3 Pour the smoothie into a tall glass and serve immediately, decorated with a sprinkling of toasted coconut.

95 Kcals

vit C

boost

Blueberry and mint

The addition of mint to this delightful low-carb smoothie makes it a most refreshing drink.

1 Put the blueberries in a blender and add the milk. Pull the mint leaves off their stalks, reserving a few sprigs for decoration, and add them to the blender. Process until smooth.

2 Pour the smoothie into a tall glass and serve immediately, decorated with the reserved sprigs of mint.

Makes 250 ml (8 fl oz)

100 g (3½ oz) frozen **blueberries**

150 ml (¼ pint) **soya milk**

small bunch **mint**

78
Kcals

vit C

revive

Apple and avocado

Makes 200 ml (7 fl oz)

1 small **avocado**

100 ml (3½ fl oz)
apple juice

2–3 **ice cubes**

slices of **apple**, to serve
(optional)

This creamy smoothie makes a delicious meal replacement, and it contains useful quantities of calcium as well as plenty of vitamin C. If you feel that you need extra protein, add a raw organic egg to the blend.

1 Cut the avocado in half, remove the stone and chop the flesh. Put the apple juice in a blender, add the avocado and a couple of ice cubes and process until smooth.

2 Pour the drink into a glass and serve immediately, decorated with slices of apple, if liked.

228
Kcals

calcium

satisfy

Cranberry and mango

This fruity smoothie contains high levels of carbohydrate and calcium, making it ideal for active people.

1 Peel the mango, remove the stone and roughly chop the flesh. Put the flesh in a blender, add the cranberry juice and yogurt and process it all until smooth.

2 Pour the smoothie into a tall glass, add a couple of ice cubes and serve immediately, decorated with slices of mango, if liked.

Makes 400 ml (14 fl oz)

1 ripe **mango**, plus extra to serve (optional)

200 ml (7 fl oz) **cranberry juice**

150 g (5 oz) **peach yogurt**

ice cubes

280 Kcals

vit C

revive

Cranberry and apple

Makes 200 ml (7 fl oz)

250 g (8 oz) **apple**

100 g (3½ oz) frozen **cranberries**

100 g (3½ oz) **natural yogurt**

1 tablespoon **clear honey**

ice cubes

All the ingredients in this drink have anti-bacterial properties. The honey will add some sweetness to the sharp taste of the cranberries.

1 Chop the apples and juice them (including the pips).

2 Transfer the apple juice to a blender, add the cranberries, yogurt and honey and process it all until smooth.

3 Pour the smoothie into a tall glass over ice and serve immediately.

339 Kcals

calcium

boost

Parsnip and pineapple

Despite the parsnips and carrots, this is a sweet, dairy-free milkshake that aids digestion and is full of protein, calcium and vitamin C.

1 Scrub the carrots and parsnips. Remove the skin and tough core from the pineapple and cut the flesh into chunks. Juice the carrots and parsnips with the pineapple.

2 Transfer the juice to a blender, add the milk and a couple of ice cubes and process until smooth.

3 Pour the smoothie into a tall glass and serve immediately, decorated with pineapple wedges, if liked.

Makes 200 ml (7 fl oz)

100 g (3½ oz) **carrots**

100 g (3½ oz) **parsnips**

250 g (8 oz) **pineapple**, plus extra to serve (optional)

75 ml (3 fl oz) **soya milk**

ice cubes

266
Kcals

calcium

soothe

Rhubarb
and custard

Makes 400 ml (14 fl oz)

150 g (5 oz) can **rhubarb**

150 g (5 oz) carton **ready-made custard**

100 ml (3½ fl oz) ice-cold **semi-skimmed milk**

1 teaspoon **icing sugar** (optional)

ice cubes (optional)

Rhubarb is a great source of potassium and also contains vitamin C and manganese. The custard and milk make this a delicious creamy drink.

1 Drain the rhubarb, put it in a blender with the custard, milk and icing sugar (if used) and process until smooth.

2 Pour the smoothie into a glass, add a couple of ice cubes, if liked, and serve immediately.

135 Kcals

vit C

satisfy

218 smoothies

Prune, apple and cinnamon

Prunes are a useful source of iron, and prune juice is a good alternative if you dislike eating whole prunes.

1 Roughly chop the prunes into small pieces. Put the prunes and cinnamon in a large bowl, pour in the apple juice, cover and leave to stand overnight.

2 Transfer the prunes and apple juice to a blender, add the yogurt and process until smooth.

3 Pour the smoothie into a tall glass over ice and serve immediately with a sprinkling of cinnamon.

Makes 400 ml (14 fl oz)

65 g (2½ oz) ready-to-eat **prunes**

pinch of **ground cinnamon**, plus extra to serve

350 ml (12 fl oz) **apple juice**

3 tablespoons **Greek yogurt**

ice cubes

270 Kcals

iron

energize

Mango and blackcurrant

Makes 780 ml (27 fl oz)

3 **mangoes**

2 tablespoons **mango sorbet**

100 ml (3½ fl oz) **apple juice**

200 g (7 oz) **blackcurrants**

This smoothie is so thick you might need a spoon to eat it, making it a delightful summer dessert. Try layering the mango and blackcurrant in an ice-lolly container to make a cooling burst of fruity goodness.

1 Peel the mangoes, remove the stones and chop the flesh into chunks. Put the mangoes, mango sorbet and half the apple juice in a blender and process briefly. Chill the purée.

2 Put the blackcurrants and the rest of the apple juice in the blender and process until smooth.

3 Spoon the mango purée into 2 glasses. Carefully pour on the blackcurrant purée to form a second layer. Drag a teaspoon or skewer down the inside of the glass to make vertical stripes around the glass. Serve immediately.

390 Kcals

vit C

satisfy

Banana and fig

These fruits are high in natural sugars, meaning they produce a feeling of fullness, which can help prevent overeating.

1 Scrub the carrots. Peel and roughly chop the ginger. Juice the figs and orange with the carrots and ginger.

2 Transfer the juice to a blender, add the banana and a couple of ice cubes and process until smooth.

3 Pour the drink into a tall glass, add more ice cubes and serve immediately, decorated with sliced figs, if liked.

Makes 200 ml (7 fl oz)

250 g (8 oz) **carrots**

2.5 cm (1 inch) cube **fresh root ginger**

100 g (3½ oz) **figs**, plus extra to serve (optional)

1 **orange**

100 g (3½ oz) **banana**

ice cubes

460 Kcals

vit A

calm

Raspberry
milkshake

Makes 200 ml (7 fl oz)

100 g (3½ oz) fresh or frozen **raspberries**

150 ml (¼ pint) **soya milk**

This soya milkshake is both delicious and incredibly healthy. Raspberries and soya beans contain health-boosting nutrients which are reported to help prevent the growth of certain cancerous cells.

1 If you are using fresh raspberries, freeze them for at least 2 hours or overnight.

2 Put the frozen raspberries in a blender, reserving 2–3 whole berries for decoration, add the milk and process until smooth.

3 Pour the smoothie into a tall glass and serve immediately, decorated with the reserved raspberries.

87 Kcals

calcium

soothe

Banana and peanut butter

Peanut butter might sound an unusual ingredient for a smoothie, but it combines wonderfully well with bananas to make a rich, satisfying drink.

1 Peel and slice the banana and freeze for at least 2 hours or overnight.

2 Put the frozen banana, milk and peanut butter or tahini paste in a blender and process until smooth. Serve immediately.

Makes 400 ml (14 fl oz)

1 ripe **banana**

300 ml (½ pint) **semi-skimmed milk**

1 tablespoon smooth **peanut butter** or 2 teaspoons **tahini paste**

326 Kcals

calcium

energize

Papaya and passion fruit

Makes 200 ml (7 fl oz)

1 **papaya**

1 **passion fruit**

juice of ½ **lime**

ice cubes

Papaya is full of enzymes and has valuable anti-parasitic qualities, while the lime juice and passion fruit provide plenty of zingy flavour.

1 Cut the papaya in half, and scoop out and discard the seeds and skin. Chop the flesh roughly and put it in a blender. Cut the passion fruit in half and spoon the juice and seeds into the blender. Add the lime juice and a couple of ice cubes and process it all until smooth.

2 Pour the drink into a tall glass and serve immediately.

65 Kcals

vit C

revive

Watermelon and strawberry

This drink can be served as a smoothie or you could make it into an iced snack. The addition of mint leaves works well, or you could try tarragon to give an unusual twist.

1 Remove the skin and, if you want, the seeds from the watermelon and chop the flesh into chunks. Hull and roughly chop the strawberries. Freeze the melon and strawberries for at least 2 hours or overnight.

2 Put the frozen watermelon and strawberries in a blender with the water, add the mint or tarragon and process until smooth.

3 Pour the purée into 2 glass tumblers, decorate with sprigs of mint or tarragon and serve immediately.

Makes 300 ml (½ pint)

100 g (3½ oz) **watermelon**

100 g (3½ oz) **strawberries**

100 ml (3½ fl oz) **water**

small handful of **mint** or **tarragon**, plus extra to serve

64 Kcals

vit C

refresh

Vanilla
and lychee

Makes 200 ml (7 fl oz)

50 g (2 oz) can **lychees**, in water or their own juice

30 g (1¼ oz) vanilla-flavoured **whey protein powder**

100 ml (3½ fl oz) sparkling **mineral water**

ice cubes

The lychees add a delicate sweetness to this protein shake, while the sparkling water gives it lightness. As well as useful amounts of vitamin C, it provides calcium and magnesium.

1 Put the lychees and the juice or water into a blender, add the whey protein powder, water and a couple of ice cubes and process until smooth.

2 Pour the drink into a tall glass and serve immediately.

 120 Kcals

 calcium

 calm

Mandarin
and lychee

Always make sure that fruit is canned in water or in its own juice, because sugar-laden syrup is full of carbs. Lychees, which are usually available canned or bottled, are a good source of vitamin C.

1 Put the mandarin oranges and the lychees together with their juices into a blender, add a couple of ice cubes and process until smooth and frothy.

2 Pour the drink into a glass and serve immediately.

Makes 150 ml (¼ pint)

100 g (3½ oz) can **mandarin oranges**, in water or their own juice

50 g (2 oz) can **lychees**, in water or their own juice

ice cubes

61 Kcals

vit C

refresh

Cucumber lassi

Makes 400 ml (14 fl oz)

150 g (5 oz)
cucumber, peeled

150 g (5 oz)
natural yogurt

100 ml (3½ fl oz)
iced **water**

handful **mint** leaves

½ teaspoon
ground cumin

squeeze **lemon juice**

Lassi is a traditional Indian drink that is served chilled. This drink is a perfect accompaniment to a spicy Indian meal as it cools the palate, or you can enjoy it on its own as a satisfying summertime drink.

1 Peel the cucumber and roughly chop the flesh. Put it in a blender and add the yogurt and water.

2 Pull the mint leaves off their stalks. If you like, reserve a few leaves for garnish. Chop the remainder, put them into the blender with the cumin and lemon juice and process until smooth.

3 Pour the lassi into 2 tall glasses, garnish with the reserved mint leaves, if liked, and serve immediately.

50
Kcals

calcium

cool

Mango lassi

A splash of rosewater and a dusting of ground cardamom add an extra taste sensation to this mango version.

1 Peel and remove the stone from the mango and cut the flesh into chunks.

2 Put the mango in a blender, add the yogurt, water, rosewater and ground cardamom (if used) and process until smooth.

3 Pour the lassi into a tall glass and serve immediately.

Makes 225 ml (7½ fl oz)

1 small **mango**

85 g (3¼ oz) **natural yogurt**

75 ml (3 fl oz) iced **water**

1 tablespoon **rosewater** (optional)

¼ teaspoon **ground cardamom** (optional)

81 Kcals

calcium

refresh

Cucumber and mint lassi

Makes 300 ml (½ pint)

about 200 g (7 oz) **cucumber**

250 g (8 oz) **natural yogurt**

handful chopped **mint**, plus extra to serve (optional)

¼ teaspoon **salt** (optional)

ice cubes

This refreshing and summery drink contains a large amount of calcium, essential for bone health, while the cucumber's high water content makes it a good choice for quenching the thirst.

1 Cut the cucumber in half lengthways and use a teaspoon to remove and discard the seeds. Roughly chop the flesh.

2 Put the cucumber in a blender, add the yogurt, mint and salt (if used) and process until smooth.

3 Pour the lassi into a glass, add a couple of ice cubes and serve immediately, garnished with mint, if liked.

220 Kcals

calcium

refresh

Strawberry and raspberry

A daily helping of strawberries can help keep your heart healthy and may also help with anti-ageing, and they contain the same disease-fighting antioxidants as raspberries.

1 Hull the strawberries. Put all the berries, milk, yogurt and rosewater in a blender and process until smooth.

2 Pour into a tall glass, stir in the honey and serve immediately, decorated with slices of strawberry.

Makes 300 ml (½ pint)

50 g (2 oz) mixed **strawberries and raspberries**

125 ml (4 fl oz) chilled **milk**

125 ml (4 fl oz) chilled **natural yogurt**

1 teaspoon **rosewater**

½ teaspoon **clear honey**

strawberry slices, to serve

150 Kcals

vit C

revive

Strawberry lassi

Makes 1.5 litres
(2½ pints)

400 g (13 oz)
strawberries

750 ml (1¼ pints)
ice-cold water

300 ml (½ pint) low-fat
natural yogurt

25 g (1 oz) **golden
caster sugar**

a few drops **rosewater**

coarsely ground **black
pepper**, to serve

A cool, creamy lassi is enjoyed throughout India,
where it is served either salty or sweet. This sweet
version is absolutely delicious. High levels of
dietary fibre mean that strawberries are good for
cleansing the digestive system.

1 Hull and roughly chop the strawberries. Put the
strawberries in a food processor with half the water
and process until smooth.

2 Add the yogurt, sugar, remaining water
and rosewater and process again until smooth
and frothy.

3 Pour into chilled, tall glasses, sprinkle with
black pepper and serve immediately.

99 Kcals

vit C

cleanse

Kiwifruit, grape and lime

It is believed that kiwifruit can help with respiratory-related disorders. The lime in this smoothie adds a refreshing, zingy burst of flavour.

1 Peel the kiwifruit and put the flesh in a blender with the grape juice and lime juice. Process until smooth.

2 Pour into glasses over ice and serve immediately, decorated with slices of kiwifruit, if liked.

Makes 575 ml (18 fl oz)

250 g (8 oz) **kiwifruit**, plus extra to serve (optional)

300 ml (½ pint) **white grape juice**

juice of 2 **limes**

ice cubes

123 Kcals

vit C

refresh

Watermelon
and citrus

Makes 4.3 litres
(7½ pints)

1 large (or 2 small) ripe
chilled **watermelon**

300 ml (½ pint)
orange juice

juice of 1 **lime**

caster sugar, to taste

slices of **lime**, to decorate
(optional)

ice cubes

Like cantaloupe melons, watermelons are a good
source of vitamin C and beta-carotene. This is
beautiful summer drink.

1 Cut the watermelon into chunks, remove the skin
and seeds and roughly chop the flesh. Put the
melon in a blender with the orange and lime juices
and process until smooth.

2 Add sugar to taste and pour into glasses over ice.
Add a slice of lime to the rim of each glass, if liked.

847
Kcals

vit C

uplift

Mango, coconut and lime lassi

Mangoes are good for the digestive system and useful for soothing indigestion. Their detoxifying properties mean they are good for cleansing the kidneys and blood and can help improve skin texture.

1 Peel the mango, remove the stone and dice the flesh. Put the mango in a blender with the orange and lime juices, honey, yogurt and coconut milk. Process until smooth.

2 Pour into tall glasses over ice and serve immediately, decorated with slices of orange, if liked.

Makes 600 ml (1 pint)

1 large ripe **mango**

juice of 1 **orange**

juice of 1 **lime**

1 tablespoon **clear honey**

300 ml (½ pint) **plain yogurt**

4 tablespoons **coconut milk**

orange slices, to decorate (optional)

ice cubes

179 Kcals

vit A

detox

Mango, banana and orange

Makes 300 ml (½ pint)

1 **mango**

1 **banana**

juice of 1 **orange**

1 dash **lime** juice

ice cubes

lime slices, to serve (optional)

Recent research has linked a citrus-rich diet with a reduced risk of some types of cancer – a great reason to try out this yummy smoothie.

1 Peel the mango, remove the stone and dice the flesh. Peel the banana and put it in a blender with the mango and juices. Process until smooth.

2 Pour into a tall glass over ice and serve immediately, decorated with slices of lime, if liked.

200 Kcals

vit C

revive

Peach, pear and raspberry

Like apples, pears are great for ridding the body of toxins, and a detoxification programme of pears alone for a day or so will deep cleanse your digestive system and work wonders for your skin.

1 Peel, core and chop the pear. Skin, stone and chop the peach. Put the raspberries, pear, peach and peach juice in a blender with a couple of ice cubes and process until smooth.

2 Pour into a tall glass and serve immediately, decorated with slices of pear, if liked.

Makes 400 ml (14 fl oz)

1 ripe **pear**, plus extra to serve (optional)

1 ripe **peach**

125 g (4 oz) **raspberries**

ice cubes

7 measures **peach juice**

160 Kcals

vit K

cleanse

Marbled peach milkshake

Makes 900 ml (1½ pints)

300 g (10 oz) **raspberries**

4 teaspoons **clear honey**

2 large juicy **peaches**

1 teaspoon **vanilla bean paste**

125 ml (4 fl oz) **single cream**

150 ml (¼ pint) **orange juice**

A great choice when you want to have something that tastes really indulgent but also contains plenty of vitamins and nutrients.

1 Put the raspberries in a blender and process to make a smooth purée. Press this through a non-metallic strainer to remove the seeds, and stir in half the honey. Check the sweetness, adding a little more honey, if liked.

2 Halve the peaches and remove the stones, then coarsely chop the flesh. Blend the peaches to a purée with the vanilla bean paste and cream. Blend in the orange juice and any remaining honey.

3 Spoon a layer of the peach purée to a depth of about 15 mm (¾ inch) in 2 glasses. Add a layer of raspberry puree and repeat the layering. Lightly marble the 2 colours together with a knife and serve.

280 Kcals

vit C

satisfy

Vanilla yogurt smoothie

Honey is a better sweetener than refined sugar as it has less effect on blood sugar levels. Remember, though, that honey is high in calories, so use it in moderation.

1 Put the yogurt, vanilla bean paste and honey in a blender and process until evenly combined.

2 With the machine running, gradually add the apple juice until the mixture is foamy on top.

3 Pour into glasses over ice and serve immediately.

Makes 500 ml (17 fl oz)

175 ml (6 fl oz) **natural yogurt**

1 teaspoon **vanilla bean paste**

2 tablespoons **clear honey**

300 ml (½ pint) **apple juice**

ice cubes

178 Kcals

vit C

energize

Blackcurrant and raspberry

Makes 450 ml (¾ pint)

150 g (5 oz)
blackcurrants or
blackberries

150 g (5 oz) raspberry or
blackberry **sorbet**

150 ml (¼ pint)
natural yogurt

4 tablespoons
single cream

2 tablespoons
clear honey

1 teaspoon
vanilla extract

This cooling drink is perfect for fruit and berry lovers and the natural ingredients make for a healthy smoothie.

1 If you are using blackcurrants, remove any stray stalks. Reserve a few pieces of fruit for decoration and put the remainder in a blender and process, scraping any pieces down from the sides of the bowl if necessary.

2 Blend again until perfectly smooth, add the sorbet and blend again to combine. Spoon the purée into 2 glasses.

3 Put the yogurt in a bowl and stir in the cream, honey and vanilla extract until evenly combined. Spoon over the fruit mixture and serve immediately, decorated with the reserved fruit.

290 Kcals

vit C

refresh

Apple and oat smoothie

Numerous studies have shown that a daily helping of oats is an excellent way of protecting the heart. They also add an interesting texture to this scrumptious smoothie.

1 Peel, core and chop the apple. Peel the banana and put it in a blender with the rest of the ingredients and process until smooth.

2 Pour into a tall glass and serve immediately.

Makes 450 ml (¾ pint)

1 **apple**

1 small **banana**

150 ml (¼ pint) low-fat **natural yogurt**

200 ml (7 fl oz) **skimmed milk**

few drops of **vanilla extract**

2 teaspoons **clear honey**

2 tablespoons **muesli**

430 Kcals

vit B

boost

Whey
and berries

Makes 250 ml (8 fl oz)

50 g (2 oz) frozen **mixed berries**, such as raspberries, strawberries, blackberries

25 g (1 oz) micro-filtered **whey protein powder**

ice cubes

still **mineral water**

To make a plain whey smoothie, simply omit the berries. If you aren't used to the taste of whey powder, try adding a little natural vanilla extract.

1 Put the frozen berries, whey protein powder and a couple of ice cubes in a blender with about 2.5 cm (1 inch) of the water and process for about 20 seconds until smooth and creamy.

2 Pour into a glass, adding more water if you want a thinner drink, and serve immediately.

100 Kcals

vit C

revive

Papaya
and soya

Papaya is the ideal fruit to start the day. Either eat it simply cut in half with a squeeze of lime on top, the seeds scooped out and discarded, or use it, as here, in a quick smoothie, which can be drunk while you get ready for the day ahead.

1 Halve the papaya, scoop out and discard the seeds and add the flesh to a blender. Peel and chop the bananas and add them to the blender with the yogurt. Process for 1 minute until smooth and frothy.

2 Add the soya milk or apple juice to the blender and process again.

3 Pour the smoothie into tall glasses over ice and serve immediately.

Makes 1 litre (1¾ pints)

1 **papaya**

2 **bananas**

300 ml (½ pint) low-fat **yogurt**

300 ml (½ pint) **soya milk** or **apple juice**

ice cubes

270
Kcals

vit A

boost

Wheatgerm and banana

Makes 1 litre (1¾ pints)

2 tablespoons
wheatgerm

1 tablespoon
sesame seeds

2 **bananas**

75 g (3 oz)
pineapple pieces

450 ml (¾ pint)
apple juice

300 ml (½ pint)
natural yogurt

Try to eat wheatgerm every day. It is a highly concentrated source of nutrients, including protein, a number of B vitamins, folic acid, vitamin E, zinc, selenium, iron and magnesium.

1 Spread the wheatgerm and sesame seeds over a baking sheet and toast gently under a preheated grill, stirring a couple of times until the sesame seeds have begun to turn a golden-brown colour. Remove from the grill and leave to cool.

2 Peel and slice the bananas. Remove the skin and the tough core from the pineapple and chop the flesh. Put the bananas and pineapple in a blender and process to a rough purée.

3 Add the apple juice and blend again to make a smooth juice. Add the yogurt and the cooled wheatgerm and sesame seeds, blend once again. Pour into tall glasses and serve.

158 Kcals

folic acid

energize

Apple and strawberry cup

In addition to vitamin C, strawberries are a good source of antioxidants. This is a sweet and fizzy drink that is a real pick-me-up.

1 Hull the strawberries, put them in a bowl and bruise them with a wooden spoon. Sprinkle over the sugar and orange juice, cover and leave to stand for 1 hour.

2 Pour the fruit cup into a jug, top it up with sparkling apple juice and ice cubes and serve immediately.

Makes 750 ml (1¼ pints)

500 g (1 lb) very ripe **strawberries**

2 tablespoons **caster sugar**

juice of 1 large **orange**

sparkling **apple juice**

ice cubes

350 Kcals

vit C

revive

Banana lassi

Makes 1.2 litres (2 pints)

3 ripe **bananas**

500 ml (17 fl oz)
natural yogurt

250 ml (8 fl oz)
ice-cold **water**

1–2 tablespoons
caster sugar

¼ teaspoon ground
cardamom seeds

Although bananas are best known as a good source of potassium, they also contain vitamin B6, which helps protect against heart disease, regulate the nervous system and promote healthy skin.

1 Peel and roughly chop the bananas and put them in a blender with the yogurt, water, caster sugar and cardamom seeds. Process until smooth.

2 Pour into tall glasses and serve immediately.

340 Kcals

vit B

satisfy

Mango and mint sherbet

The antioxidant vitamins A, C and E in mangoes have powerful immunity-boosting properties, giving you a health boost while you enjoy this taste of paradise!

1 Peel and stone the mangoes and roughly chop the flesh. Put it in a blender with the lemon juice, sugar, mint leaves and water and process it all until smooth.

2 Pour into glasses over ice and serve immediately.

Makes 1.5 litres (2½ pints)

3 ripe **mangoes**

4 tablespoons **lemon juice**

1 tablespoon **caster sugar**

12 **mint** leaves, finely chopped

900 ml (1½ pints) ice-cold **water**

ice cubes

340 Kcals

vit C

boost

Peaches and sunflower

Makes 300 ml (½ pint)

200 ml (7 fl oz) can
peaches in grape juice,
plus extra to serve
(optional)

100 ml (3½ fl oz)
soya milk

15 g (½ oz)
sunflower seeds

ice cubes

At times when you are too busy to buy fresh fruit,
make this reviving drink from a few store-cupboard
ingredients.

1 Put the peaches and their juice in a blender with
the soya milk and sunflower seeds and process for
about 20 seconds until smooth. Add a few ice cubes
and blend again for about 10 seconds.

2 Pour into 2 glasses over ice and serve
immediately, decorated with slices of peach, if liked.

199 Kcals

amino acids

revive

Apricot and nectarine

This wonderful golden drink is full of beta-carotene, vitamin C and iron. The vitamin C helps the absorption of the iron, which makes it an ideal choice for anyone feeling a little below par.

1 Cut the apricots and nectarine or peach in half and remove the stones. Chop the flesh. Cut the passion fruit in half, scoop out the pulp and strain it through a sieve to remove the seeds.

2 Put the apple juice in a blender with the apricot, nectarine or peach, passion fruit and a couple of ice cubes and process until smooth.

3 Pour into glasses and serve immediately.

Makes 400 ml (14 fl oz)

3 **apricots**

1 large **nectarine** or **peach**

2 **passion fruit**

150 ml (¼ pint) **apple juice**

ice cubes

180 Kcals

vit C

boost

Strawberry and cherry

Makes 600 ml (1 pint)

150 g (5 oz) **strawberries**

125 g (4 oz) **cherries**

125 g (4 oz) **watermelon**

100 ml (3½ fl oz) **orange juice**

500 ml (17 fl oz) chilled **sparkling water**

The sparkling water in this smoothie makes this an interesting choice for a non-alcoholic cocktail or long summer drink to enjoy in the garden.

1 Hull the strawberries. Halve and pit the cherries. Peel and deseed the watermelon and cut it into small chunks. Put all the fruit in a blender with the orange juice and process until smooth.

2 If you prefer a smooth drink, sieve the purée over a bowl to remove the pips, skin and seeds.

3 Pour the purée into 3 glasses, top up with the sparkling water and serve immediately.

58 Kcals

vit C

refresh

Strawberry and orange fizz

This is a healthy alternative to most commercial fizzy drinks and contains a large amount of vitamin C with hardly any calories.

1 Hull the strawberries. Put the strawberries and orange juice in a blender and process until smooth.

2 Place 1 ice cube in each of 2 glasses and add the strawberry liquid.

3 Pour the sparkling mineral water into the blender, process very briefly and use to top up the glasses. Stir briskly and serve.

Makes 325 ml (11 fl oz)

8–10 **strawberries**

125 ml (4 fl oz) **orange juice**

2 **ice cubes**

125 ml (4 fl oz) sparkling **mineral water**

105 Kcals

vit C

refresh

index

a

b

c

Executive Editor Nicky Hill

Editor Ruth Hamilton

Executive Art Editor
Darren Southern

Designer Ginny Zeal

Senior Production Controller
Manjit Sihra

Introduction supplied by
Cara Frost-Sharratt